Edward Alfred Pollard

Observations in the North

Eight Months in Prison and on Parole

Edward Alfred Pollard

Observations in the North
Eight Months in Prison and on Parole

ISBN/EAN: 9783744762441

Printed in Europe, USA, Canada, Australia, Japan

Cover: Foto ©Suzi / pixelio.de

More available books at **www.hansebooks.com**

OBSERVATIONS

ON

THE NORTH:

EIGHT MONTHS IN PRISON AND ON PAROLE.

BY

EDWARD A. POLLARD.

RICHMOND:
E. W. AYRES, CORNER NINTH AND MAIN STREETS.
1865.

PREFATORY.

The writer was captured by the enemies of his country, on his way to Europe. A brief record of his captivity may afford an exhibition of moral aspects of the war, which are, indeed, the most interesting part of its history; and what he observed in an interval of parole, extending over several months, in which time he had the opportunity of visiting the principal cities of the North, and obtaining an insight into Yankee politics and society, may have a value to those many persons in the Confederate States who desire to know the real temper and political designs of the North.

No one can justly charge the writer with attempt at any base gratification in libel or abuse in the following pages. He leaves such resources of revenge to the baser of his enemies, and he challenges every man who respects the freedom and honesty of literature, to say whether in these pages he has been insensible even to one glimpse of kindness in his prison, or has done more, on any occasion, than refuse for interest or convenience, to compromise THE TRUTH.

CONTENTS.

CHAPTER I.

Running the Blockade.—The "Greyhound."—Passing the Blockade Lines.—The Capture.—Yankee Courtesy.—Off Fortress Monroe.................................. 9

CHAPTER II.

Curiosities of the Yankee Blockade.—Correspondence with Lord Lyons, &c...... 15

CHAPTER III.

A week in Boston.—Introduction to the United States Marshal.—A Fugitive Slave.—In the Streets of Boston: Two Spectacles.—A Circle of Secessionists in the "Hub of the Universe."... 25

CHAPTER IV.

Commitment to Fort Warren.—Horrours of the Yankee Bastile.—Torture of "A Brutal Villain."—A Letter to Secretary Welles................................... 32

CHAPTER V.

Journal Notes in Prison.—Precious Tributes of Sympathy.—Portrait of the Yankee.—A New England Shepherd.—Sufferings and Reflections.—Fourth of July in Fort Warren.. 40

CHAPTER VI.

Journal Notes Continued.—Life in the Casemates.—How the Yankees Treat Foreigners.—Southern "Aristocracy."—Friends in Boston.—Massachusetts "Chivalry."—"Have we a Government?".. 46

CHAPTER VII.

Episodes in Prison.—A Council in the Casemates.—An Attempt to Escape......... 52

CHAPTER VIII.

Journal Notes.—My Affair with Lord Lyons Ended.—The Niagara Falls Bubble.—Comforting Words.—How Dying Prisoners are Treated................................. 58

CHAPTER IX.

Journal Notes Continued.—A Yankee's Confession: Confederate Civilization.—A "Map of Busy Life" in Boston.— ...... Sickness and Reflections in Prison: Female Philosophy on the War.. 63

CHAPTER X.

Out of Prison.—My Parole.—My Boston Benefactress.—In Yankee Atmosphere.—A Letter from Boston.—Some Words on "Peace Negotiations."—Waiting...... 68

CHAPTER XI.

Parties and Opinions in the North.—Vagabond Knights of Secessia................. 73

CHAPTER XII.

The True Value of the Military Situation in the North.—The Question of Endurance on the part of the Confederacy.. 80

CHAPTER XIII.

Journal Notes.—Letter from a Catholic Friend.—An Evening Party in Brooklyn.—Political Preaching.—Renegade Virginians................................. 86

CHAPTER XIV.

A Comparative View of Northern Despotism.—The Record of Mr. Lincoln's Administration... 92

CHAPTER XV.

From New York to Fortress Monroe.—Two Days in Baltimore.—A Bit of Romance.—Captain "Puffer."—The Negro Settlement at Fortress Monroe 93

CHAPTER XVI.

A Day with General Butler.—The Civilization and Poetry of the "Sanitary Commission."—General Butler's Philosophy and "Little Stories." 104

CHAPTER XVII.

On Parole in Fortress Monroe.—A Recollection of General Fitz Lee.—A Bitter Disappointment.—Letter from a Catholic Mother: *In Memoriam* 113

CHAPTER XVIII.

Close and Solitery Confinement.—Life in a Guard-Box.—Memorable Sufferings.— A Glimpse of Hope 117

CHAPTER XIX.

A Week in the Yankee Lines around Richmond.—The Pleasure Party on the "River Queen."—General Butler Aroused and Profane.—Yankee "War Correspondents" at Headquarters.—Material of the Yankee Army: Negro Soldiers.—Yankee Officers on "Subjugation."—General Butler's Tribute to General Lee.—How I Made a Narrow Escape to Richmond............................. 123

CHAPTER XX.

Some Reflections.—The Hope of the Confederacy............................. 131

CHAPTER I.

RUNNING THE BLOCKADE.—The "Greyhound."—Passing the Blockade Lines.—The Capture.—Yankee Courtesy.—Off Fortress Monroe.

"Running the Blockade" to Europe is a pleasant thought to one in Richmond: the imagination of an adventure at the end of which are golden visions and that beatitude which may be summed up in "plenty to wear and to eat." The first stage of the adventure brings one to Wilmington; and here he already finds in the luxurious cabins of the blockade-runners the creature-comforts to which he has long been a stranger in the Confederate capital, and has a foretaste of some of the sweets of his adventure.

Oranges, which, if they existed in Richmond, would be ticketed in some Jew's window at twenty dollars apiece; pineapples, with their forgotten fragrance; wines and liquors, of which we have only the poisoned imitations in Richmond; and an array of cut and stained glass-ware that would have put to blush the stock of all the hotels in the Confederacy (I had been eating and drinking out of tin at the Wilmington hotel,) were set out with a bewildering profusion in the cabin of the "Greyhound," when I called to make my respects to Captain "Henry" and conclude my arrangements for passage out to Bermuda. What a splendid fellow he was: a graceful dash of manner, which yet beamed with intelligence, an exuberant hospitality, a kindness that when it did a grateful thing so gracefully waived all expressions of obligation. He had been all over the world; was familiar with the great capitals of Europe; bore the marks of a wound obtained in the campaign of Stonewall Jackson; and as to his name and nationality—why, passengers on blockade-runners are not expected to be inquisitive of these circumstances, and must beware of impertinent curiosity.

"Want to get out on the Greyhound? Why, certainly; shall be very glad to have you;" and the Captain blew his piratical silver whistle, and his clerk had soon noted my height, colour of my eyes, &c., for the Confederate officer, who was to come aboard next morning to muster crew and passengers, and see that no conscripts made an unticketed exit from Wilmington.

The reader must understand that, on vessels running the blockade, there is no accommodation for passengers, unless in the contracted space of the captain's own cabin; hence, passengers are taken only by extraordinary favour.

What a contrast was the ready consent of Captain "Henry," an entire stranger, to the negatives and quibbles of others. For there are in Wilmington specimens of the Southern Yankee: men, as we have seen them in Richmond, whose swollen wealth, and beefy vulgarity, and insatiable avarice, number them with that brood of moral bastardy. Two officers of the volunteer navy of the Confederacy, who desired passage to proceed to a most important rendezvous, in urgent interests of the public service, were ruthlessly disappointed, because they could not manage to pay, for a seventy hours' passage to Bermuda, four hundred dollars in gold—then eight thousand dollars in the currency of the Confederacy.*

On the night of the 9th of May, 1864, the Greyhound was lying off Fort Fisher, the signal-men blinking at each other with their lights in sliding boxes. It was necessary to get a dispensation from the fort for the Greyhound to pass out to sea, as no less than three fugitive conscripts—"stowaways"—had been found aboard of her. Two of them were discovered on searching the vessel at Wilmington. But lower down the stream the vessel is overhauled again, and goes through the process of the *fumigation* of her hold to discover improper passengers In the case of the Greyhound, to the intense disgust of the captain, and execrations of the crew, the process brought to light an unhappy stowaway, who was recognized as a liquor-dealer of Wilmington, and made no secret of his design to flee the conscription. After the threat, and apparently serious preparations, to throw him overboard, the "stowaway" was, no doubt, relieved to find himself taken ashore to the comparative mercies of the enrolling officer.

---

* I had been very kindly offered by Governour Vance, of North Carolina, a passage on the line of steamers run by that State. There was no boat of that line then in port. I asked a Richmond man, largely interested in blockade-running, who is known to have accumulated vast wealth by the Davis patronage in Richmond, and to have fattened on the marrow-bones of the Commissary Department, the very small favour of allowing me a passage in one of his boats, in consideration that my pass on the North Carolina line might be transferred to any other passenger he might hereafter name on his own account—in fact, nothing more than a simple exchange of convenience. I got a flat and boorish refusal. Yet, a British vessel took me out; and her captain, discovering my disappointment, and understanding the object of my proposed visit to England, placed his cabin at my disposal, and refused to take anything in return for his kindness but my thanks.

At last we are off. The moon is down; the steward has had orders to kill the geese and shut up the dog; the captain has put on a suit of dark clothes; every light is extinguished, every word spoken in a whisper, and the turn of the propeller of the Greyhound sounds like the beat of a human heart. There is an excitement in these circumstances. The low, white gray vessel glides furtively through the water, and you catch the whispered commands of the captain: "Stead-ey," and then the more intense and energetic whisper: "Black smoke, by G—; cut off your smoke." Every eye is strained into the shadows of the night. But how utterly useless did all this precaution and vigilance appear on the Greyhound; for after two hours of suspense we were out of the blockade lines, and had seen nothing but the caps of the waves. A blockade for blockheads, surely, I thought, as I composed myself to sleep, dismissing entirely from my mind all terrors of the Yankee.

It was about two o'clock the next day, and the Greyhound was about one hundred and fifty miles out at sea, when the lookout reported a steamer astern of us. The day was hazy, and when the vessel was first descried, she could not have been more than five or six miles astern of us. For a few moments there was a sharp suspense; perhaps the steamer had not seen us; every one listened with breathless anxiety, as the tall fellow at the mast-head reported the discoveries he was making, through his glasses, of the suspicious vessel. "He is bearing towards a bark, sir;" and for a few moments hope mounted in our hearts that we might not have been observed, and might yet escape into the misty obscurity of the sea. In vain. "He is a side-wheel steamer, and is bearing directly for us, sir." "Give her her way," shouted the captain in response; and there was a tumultuous rush of the crew to the engine-room, and the black smoke curling above the smoke-stack and the white foam in our wake told plainly enough that the startled Greyhound was making desperate speed.

But she was evidently no match for the Yankee. We were being rapidly overhauled, and in something more than an hour from the beginning of the chase a shell from the Yankee vessel, the "Connecticut," was whistling over our bows. The crew became unruly; but Captain "Henry," revolver in hand, ordered back the man to the wheel, declaring "he was master of the vessel yet." The mate reported that a very small crew appeared to be aboard the Yankee. "Then we will fight for it," said the spunky captain. But the madness of such a resolution became soon manifest: for as the Connecticut overhauled us more closely, her decks and wheel-houses were seen to be black with men, and a shell, which grazed our engine, warned us that we were at the mercy of the enemy. But for that peculiar nuisance of blockade-runners—women passengers—the Greyhound might have been burnt, and the last duty performed in the face of the rapacious enemy.

Dizzy, and disgusted with sea-sickness; never supposing that a vessel which had passed out of the asserted lines of blockade without seeing a blockader, without being pursued from those lines, and already far out on the sacred highway of the ocean, and flying the British ensign, could be the subject of piratical seizure; never dreaming that a simple Confederate passenger could be the victim of *kidnapping* on the high seas, outside of all military and territorial lines, I had but a dim appreciation of the excited scenes on the Greyhound in the chase. Papers, memoranda, packages of Confederate bonds, were ruthlessly tossed into the purser's bag to be consumed by the flames in the engine-room; the contents of trunks were wildly scattered over the decks; the white waves danced with ambrotypes, souvenirs, and the torn fragments of the large package of letters, missives of friendship, records of affection, which had been entrusted to me, and which I at last unwillingly gave to the sea.

Here, at last, close alongside of us, in the bright day, was the black, guilty thing, while from her sides were pushing out boats, with well-dressed crews in lustrous uniforms and officers in the picturesqueness of gold and blue—a brave sight for grimy Confederates! The Greyhound was no sooner boarded, than an ensign, who had his hair parted in the middle, and his hands encased in lavender-colored kids, came up to me and asked me with a very joyous air how many bales of cotton were on board the vessel. I afterwards understood that, from my disconsolate looks, he had taken me to be the owner of the cotton, and was probably desirous, by his amiable question, to give a sly pinch to my misery.

These plain records of experience, which are memorable in my life, would have no value for me, and would, indeed, be despicable scribblings, if they did not contain the truth. Where there is any fact in these experiences to the enemy's credit I shall not suppress it; he shall not only have the benefit of it, but my grateful acknowledgments; for I am too proud of the reputation of Confederates for candour and sensibility to kindness to risk it for the miserable gratification of writing a libel for popular passion.

I shall ever retain a pleasant and grateful recollection of the treatment I, in common with all the prisoners, obtained on board the Connecticut, and the humane courtesy of her commander, John J. Almy. I had all the accommodations and attentions usually given to a passenger, was provided with a stateroom, took my meals in the ward-room, and—what was the most grateful surprise of all—never had my ear assailed with the epithet of "rebel," or any of the dirty phrases which I had supposed to be common in Yankee conversation whenever it alluded to the Confederacy. I was told by those who had more experience in the matter than myself that the officers of the *old* navy of the United States are remarkable for their decorous manners towards prisoners, and, in this respect, presented a striking contrast to the coarse vulgarity of the Yankee army.

On the bright twelfth of May, the Connecticut was moving up the estuary of the James from Fortress Monroe to Newport News. The men-of-war and ironclads which thronged the stream afforded an exhibition of the enemy's naval power, which made us smile to think how little all this brave show of ribbed guns and armaments had accomplished against the stark spirit and beggarly resources of those who fight for liberty.

The pilot who boarded us off the Capes (a fellow with a bilious skin and greased hair, who claimed to be from Maryland), brought a wonderful story of the progress of the war in Virginia. "The New York *Herald* had news as big as his fist: Beauregard's army cut in two; Lee on a foot-race to Richmond; ahead, everywhere," etc. I had heard such stuff before, and having had some experience of dissecting Yankee lies with pen and scissors, was not easily imposed upon by the pilot's resurrection of such from the columns of New York journals.

At our mess in the ward-room, a fellow-prisoner was tempted to ask the pilot if there were any Virginia pilots employed in the bay or river. "Not one," was the fellow's reply; and a flush of shame might have passed his cheek on observing the proud and meaning glance which three of the prisoners, Virginians, exchanged at the announcement. I had heard before that the Virginia pilots, without a solitary exception, had abandoned their livelihoods and professions, spurning the temptations of the enemy and the gains they might have made from dishonour; but here was the unquestionable testimony of their self-sacrifice from the lips of an enemy and a rival. I do not know that the State of Virginia has ever done anything for these noble men, turned adrift from their employment, many of them I know earning scanty bread about Richmond, by the pitiable shifts of the refugee. Surely, such sacrifices as they have made should be gratefully recognized, and, as far as possible, rewarded; for they are another public decoration of the honour of the "Old Dominion" in this war.

CHAPTER II.

CURIOSITIES OF THE YANKEE BLOCKADE.—Correspondence with Lord Lyons, &c.

My sense of the personal kindness of Captain Almy and his officers certainly did not disturb my conviction that the Connecticut had done a monstrous wrong, and that these persons were the instruments of a despotism at Washington, that, among other iniquities of the war, was imposing upon the world the monstrous lie of a blockade, which was, in fact, an ill-disguised system of piracy.

There were in my mind certain questions touching the practical conduct of that blockade, which I was satisfied had not been pressed upon the attention of European Governments; which made what lawyers call "a case" for the Greyhound, and which might possibly result, through the timely and determined protests of some one, in the rescue of the vessel from her captors. I determined to risk my liberty in the attempt to make the issue. I had my opportunity of escape in suppressing my name and keeping quiet; but my convictions of justice to the vessel, and my confidence in the eventual triumph of principles, determined me to risk my case, not on a disguise, but on the truthful grounds that myself and vessel were legally exempt from capture. I had already written to Lord Lyons claiming my release, and having resolved to make a similar issue for the vessel, I avowed to Captain Almy the necessity of my being sent to Boston, where the prize proceedings were to be held, to make the proper protests in behalf and in the interest of the owners of the Greyhound. I was sent on board the Greyhound, and soon secured the means of a free communication in my own name and that of the Captain with Lord Lyons: the result, a correspondence which must here anticipate my narrative of events. Little did I know what that correspondence was to cost me in the resentment of the Washington Government; for in it I had presumed to denounce the cheat of the blockade, and to attempt to rescue from Yankee clutches a prize worth more than half a million of dollars. What I was to endure for the temerity will follow in the course of the narrative, which the correspondence below anticipates—inserted here, if for no other interest, as an independent chapter on the curiosities of the Yankee blockade.

CORRESPONDENCE.

I.

On Board the United States Steamer Connecticut,
At Sea, May 11, 1864.

Lord Lyons, Envoy Extraordinary and Minister Plenipotentiary for her Britannic Majesty, near Washington, United States:

My Lord: I have respectfully to represent to you that I was arrested yesterday on the high seas, by the United States steamer Connecticut, from the deck of the British steamer Greyhound, in which I was a passenger for Bermuda, en route for England—the Greyhound, at the time of capture, being about one hundred and fifty miles out at sea, and flying the British ensign. Having passed out of the lines of blockade, and of contested territorial jurisdiction, my right as a passenger became, as I conceive, analagous and tantamount to those of asylum under the British flag; and, in this respect, I invoke its protection, and that I may be permitted to pursue my way to England.

I was on board the Greyhound in the simple and exclusive character of a passenger. When arrested there on the high seas I was proceeding to England to fulfil an engagement for a literary work on the Confederate States, &c., with publishers in London, who had already printed two volumes I had composed of a similar nature; and also to discharge a private and domestic duty in visiting the relatives of my wife, who is a native of England and a subject of Her Britannic Majesty. I am not connected with the military service of the Confederate States, and am charged with no public office or trust on their behalf. These facts may be readily established by appropriate evidence; and in consideration of them, I submit to your Lordship that, if interposition be necessary, I may be protected in those very obvious rights, which I invoke in the character of an innocent passenger on the high seas, under the British flag.

I have the honour, &c., your obedient servant,

EDWARD A. POLLARD.

II.

On Board British Steamer Greyhound,
New York, May 16, 1864.

Lord Lyons, Envoy Extraordinary, &c., near Washington, D. C.:

My Lord: The Greyhound, on which I am now held as a prisoner, having been ordered to Boston, and stopping here to coal, I take the opportunity to enclose to your Lordship the duplicate of a former letter, written while I was a prisoner on board the United States steamer Connecticut, and placed in the hands of Commander John J. Almy, commanding said steamer, for transmission: using the opportunity thus to insure communication.

It is, doubtless, unnecessary to encumber the statement I have already submitted to your Lordship with any argument. But there is one view of the matter which it may not be unnecessary or presumptuous to bring to your Lordship's attention.

It must frequently happen (as it has occurred in my case) that the Confederate States, from obvious considerations of military prudence, deny all communications through the United States, or other adjoining territory, by land, and that, then, the only possible mode of egress is by sea, on vessels which pass through the line of blockade. If, on board of one of these vessels, which carried the British flag, and had passed out of the jurisdiction claimed by the United States, I was not protected from arrest, then it follows that the passenger (be he Englishman or Confederate) is made the victim of a necessity which he could not avoid, and for which he is not responsible. Such a rule would involve the rights of your own countrymen, my Lord, and any passenger, whose misfortune it was that he could not get out of the Confederate States, without crossing the ocean, might be, after he had passed out of the lines of contested territorial jurisdiction, hunted on the high seas as lawful prize, and be at the mercy of any arbitrary arrest.

I did not take passage on board the Greyhound out of the port of Wilmington until I had ascertained to my satisfaction that she was a *bona fide* British vessel, having undertaken the single voyage in which she was captured under a charter party, and entitled to carry the British flag, at least so far as to protect *passengers*, subject only to the risk of capture within the territorial limit asserted by the United States. I trust that my circumspection in this matter has not been without avail, and that, having sought the protection of the British flag, in good faith, and with an innocent purpose, I may speedily realize it through the offices of your Lordship.

I have the honour to renew my respects.

Your obedient servant,
EDWARD A. POLLARD.

III.

On Board Steamer Greyhound,
At Sea, May 14, 1864.

Lord Lyons, Envoy Extraordinary, &c., for Her Britannic Majesty, near Washington, United States:

My Lord: I am now held as prisoner on board the British steamer Greyhound, which is claimed as a prize by the United States steamship Connecticut, and is ordered, as I am informed, to the port of Boston, where proceedings will be taken for her condemnation. The circumstances under which the Greyhound was captured are peculiar, and involve a question of the most obvious interest and gravest import to Her Majesty's Government and to the rights of property in her subjects.

The Greyhound was, in good faith, and in all respects, a British vessel, and had been chartered at Bermuda to take out from the port of Wilmington certain private cotton purchased and paid for by subjects of Great Britain, and held exclusively on their own account. Not one pound of this cotton belonged to any citizen of the Confederate States; nor did any such citizen have any interest whatever in the vessel or her venture. Your Lordship will be easily able to determine from the ship's papers, and all other circumstances, that the nationality of the Greyhound was not a disguise—an adopted convenience for running the blockade—but was in all respects a true and unaffected claim on the part of her owners.

At the time of the capture of the Greyhound, on the 10th instant, she was in lat. 33 degs. 10 min. 15 sec., and long. 75 degs. 47 min. 45 sec. west, one hundred and twenty-five miles from the nearest land, flying the British ensign. She had passed out to sea from the port of Wilmington without seeing a Federal cruiser, and without any visible evidence of a blockade. But even if that blockade had existed, and was something more than a vicious fiction, by which Federal cruisers, instead of picketing the coast, are permitted to take easy prizes on the high seas, I submit to your Lordship that the Greyhound, having once passed out the territorial limit, and flying the British flag, not for the purposes of concealment, but by clear title of right, could not be outlawed on the high seas, and took the risks of blockade only within the territorial jurisdiction claimed by the United States. Any other rule would extend the jurisdiction of the United States over the high seas, and the flag of Her Majesty's Government, carried there by a clear title in the vessel to fly it, would afford no protection.

As another circumstance of the illegality in the capture of the Greyhound—indeed, I may say as one of wholly unnecessary indignity—I have further to state to your Lordship, that when the vessel had been brought to Newport News, the Commodore present, the senior officer commanding the Federal squadron, commanded the British flag on my vessel to be hauled down, and the Federal flag to be hoisted in its place. There is certainly no shadow of right for such a proceeding until the vessel is condemned in due course of law; and of the spirit of an act, where the law and the rule of propriety which it equally offends are both so plain, your Lordship will doubtless have no difficulty in judging.

Trusting that the rights of the owners of the Greyhound, which I am left for the present to represent, will receive the attention of your Lordship, and having every confidence in your Lordship's sensibility to whatever touches the rights and honour of Her Majesty's Government,

I have the honour, &c.,

Your obedient servant,

GEORGE HENRY,
Master of the Greyhound.

IV.

BRITISH LEGATION,
WASHINGTON, D. C., May 20, 1864.

Sir: It is the usual and correct practice that the master and one or more of the other persons taken on board a neutral vessel captured for breach of blockade should be sent in the vessel to a port of the captor, in order that their evidence may be taken in the case; but if such persons be neutral, they ought to be released as soon as they have given their evidence, and their evidence ought to be taken without unnecessary delay.

I have written to the Secretary of State of the United States to express my hope that you will be set free immediately after your evidence has been taken; and I beg of you to lose no time in informing me if this be not done.

I have also applied to the Secretary of State of the United States for the release of those of the officers and crew of the Greyhound who were taken out of the vessel, and who have, I am sorry to say, been detained as prisoners at Camp Hamilton, near Fortress Monroe.

I am, sir, your obedient servant, LYONS.

E. A. Pollard, Esq.

V.

Boston, May 26, 1864.

Lord Lyons, Envoy Extraordinary, &c., for Her Britannic Majesty, near Washington, United States:

My Lord: I have been detained here as a prisoner one week to-day, notwithstanding the notification under date of 20th instant, with which your Lordship obliged me, to the effect that you had applied to the Secretary of State of the United States for my release.

There are two points in my case which I beg to bring to your attention again in a precise and brief recapitulation:

1. The Greyhound had passed out of the port of Wilmington, without sight of a blockading vessel, and was taken by a cruiser about one hundred and fifty miles out at sea. I desire to put the question to your Lordship, if the Government at Washington can so change its tactics of blockade as to omit an efficient guard of the coast and take up vessels which have come out of Confederate ports by fast-sailing cruisers on the ocean highway; for such I was informed, by an officer of the United States steamer Connecticut, was the recently adopted and easy plan of taking prizes, the fruits of which your Lordship may have observed in the capture of four vessels as prizes *in a single week*, each taken far out on the high seas.

2. The Greyhound was thoroughly a British vessel; the British flag she carried, was *not a decoy;* and that flag covered me *after I had passed out of the territorial jurisdiction of the United States;* and, even in case it did not protect vessel or cargo, (granting, for argument, these to be of an illicit character,) protected me as an innocent passenger; else, having no other egress from the Confederate States, the passenger would be the victim of his necessity; and, else again, if a citizen of the Confederate States, not contraband, could be outlawed on the high seas, under that flag, flying on a *bona fide* British vessel, why not a subject or citizen of any other Government? If the flag was a reality at all, it certainly should give protection on the ocean highway to a passenger who was pursuing objects of private convenience, and certainly was not amenable to any military penalties of the Government at Washington.

Begging that your Lordship will acquit me of the charge of importunity in a matter the importance of which is by no means altogether personal to myself, I have the honour, &c.,

Your obedient servant,

Edward A. Pollard.

P. S.—I telegraphed your Lordship on the 24th instant to obtain liberty for me to see you in Washington in the interest of the Greyhound, but have received no reply: hence these lines.

Another circumstance: It is true, that if the blockade-runner be seen in *flagrante delictu* passing the territorial lines, she may be pursued and taken on the high seas. But the Greyhound was not pursued: she was waylaid on the highway of the seas. Such a practice would convert the blockade into a system of roving commissions, and might as well be predicated of the coast of Bermuda as of that of the Confederate States.

VI.

British Legation, Washington, D. C.,
May 28, 1864.

Sir: I have received your letter of the day before yesterday.

On receiving your telegram of the 24th instant, stating that you were charged to represent to me the facts of the case of the Greyhound and the interests of the owners, I sent by telegraph instructions to Her Majesty's consul at Boston to ask you to communicate on these matters with him for my information. I have to-day received from him an account of an interview which he had with you the day before yesterday.

I will request the consul to see that any British subjects interested in the Greyhound have proper facilities for defending their interests before the Prize Court. This is all I can do at present. I have referred the case to Her Majesty's Government, and I deem it right to wait for instructions from them before taking further steps.

I am, sir, your obedient servant,
LYONS.

Edward A. Pollard, Esq.

VII.

Fort Warren, Boston Harbour,
July 2 [should be *June* 2], 1864.

Lord Lyons, Envoy Extraordinary and Minister Plenipotentiary for Her Britannic Majesty, near Washington:

My Lord: I have been honored by your attention in two letters, which, I beg leave to state, very respectfully, have left me in some confusion of mind as to your Lordship's views and intentions with reference to my case. On the 20th ultimo, you write that you had "expressed your hope" to the Secretary of State of the United States that I should be "set free immediately," &c.; and on the 28th ultimo, you do not say what has been the issue of that hope, and while referring to the prize proceedings against the Greyhound, you make no reference whatever to my personal claims of protection by the British flag as a passenger on the high seas. In the meantime, I have been imprisoned in Fort Warren, by orders from Washington, without notice, without trial, and without being advised of any charge whatever against me.

It is true that Her Majesty's consul at Boston mentioned to me that he understood that you had written the first letter, assuring me of my claim of liberty, under the impression that I was a British subject: an impression which your Lordship will do me the justice to observe was not derived from any statement of mine, or any implication of my correspondence. But I cannot see the force of the distinction. If I had been an Englishman, it seems I would have been entitled to my release: why?—by grace of the Washington authorities or by force of right? The former supposition, I think I may safely say, would be resented by yourself, as well as by your Government, my Lord; and if the release, then, is to be put on any grounds of right, then the case of the Englishman would be no better than my own. The flag would protect me as well as him. It either must be a piece of bunting, and protects nothing; or, if it protects anything, it would protect all *passengers* alike. As far as the question is that of citizens or persons, it belongs to my own Government, and I am willing to rest it there; but as a question involving the British flag on the high seas, which either sinks there all other insignia and distinctions of nationality, and protects all passengers alike, or is an unmeaning display, I have brought it to the consideration of your Lordship, and respectfully asked your decision. I cannot find that the latter is stated or intimated in the letters of your Lordship, to which I have had the honour to refer.

I have, etc., your obedient servant,

EDWARD A. POLLARD.

VIII.

BRITISH LEGATION, WASHINGTON, D. C.
June 9, 1864.

Sir: I received, on the 6th instant, a letter from you, dated (evidently by mistake) 2d of July. In answer to it, I can only say that I have referred your case to Her Majesty's Government, and sent them copies of your letters to me, and that, while waiting for instructions from them, I do not feel at liberty to discuss the subject. Whatever orders they may think proper to give will be immediately executed by me.

I am, sir, your obedient servant,

LYONS.

E. A. Pollard, Esq.

NOTES.

The law of blockade was early defined in this country under the pressure of the British orders in council and blockade of 1806, in retaliation for the Berlin decree, at which time we find the elaborate protests of Madison against "the mockeries and mischiefs practised under the name of blockade." The doctrine of fictitious blockade was then exploded, and Great Britain was compelled to conform her practice to the definition made in her convention with Russia in 1801, to the effect that a blockaded port was only such as there was an "evident danger in entering."

In this war the United States have gone far beyond these abuses of fictitious blockades, which she formerly made subjects of such violent complaint, and has practically converted the blockade which she asserts of the Confederate coasts into a system of roving commissions, by which vessels *not chased from the blockade lines* are waylaid and taken up by cruisers on the ocean highway. Captures, such as that of the Greyhound, are acts of *piracy*.

But, in the above correspondence, a second point is discovered. It is contended that not only was the Greyhound not a good prize, but that the taking a passenger from the shelter of her flag was an aggravation of the capture, and the plain offence of *kidnapping*.

On the second point we have American authority so decisive and abundant, that not an inch of ground is left for the Government at Washington, which still uses the style, and, of course, is bound by the precedents of the United States, whereon to defend such a violation of a neutral flag.

It was Daniel Webster who put a well-recognized principle of international law in this neat phrase: "That a ship on the high seas was part of the nation's territory." It was on this ground that the United States defended the rights of her flag against every claim which Great Britain ever made of arrest under it.

In a letter of instructions, written in 1804, by Mr. Madison, then Secretary of State, to Mr. Monroe, resident minister in London, there is a plain and complete enunciation of the doctrine contended for in the above correspondence Referring to the immunities of a neutral flag, as recognized by Great Britain, the Secretary writes:

"She will not deny the general freedom of the high seas, and of neutral vessels navigating them, with such exceptions only as are annexed to it by the law of nations. . . . *But nowhere will she find an exception to this freedom of the seas, and of neutral flags, which justifies the taking away of any person, not* an *enemy in military service, found on board a neutral vessel.* If treaties, British as well as others, are to be consulted on this subject, it will equally appear that no countenance to the practice can be found in them. Whilst they admit a contraband of war, by enumerating its articles, and the effect of a real blockade by defining it, in no instance do they **affirm** or imply a right in any sovereign *to enforce his claims to the allegiance of his subjects on board neutral vessels on the high seas;* on the contrary, whenever a **belligerent claim** against persons on board a neutral vessel is referred to in treaties, *enemies in military service alone* are excepted from the general immunity of persons in that situation; and this exception confirms the immunity of those who are not included in it. . . . If *the law of allegiance which is a municipal law,* be in force at all on the high seas on board foreign vessels, it must be so at all times there, as it is within its acknowledged sphere. If the reason alleged for it be good in time of war, namely, that the sovereign has then a right to the services of all his subjects, it must be good at all times, because he has the same right to their service. . . . Taking reason and justice for the tests of this practice, it is peculiarly indefensible, because it deprives the dearest rights of persons of a regular trial, to which the most inconsiderable article of property captured on the high seas is entitled, and leaves their destiny to the will of an officer." (Am. State Papers. Vol. III. Foreign Relations, p. 84.)

CHAPTER III.

A WEEK IN BOSTON.—Introduction to the U. S. Marshal.—A Fugitive Slave.—In the Streets of Boston: Two Spectacles.—A Circle of Secessionists in the "Hub of the Universe."

As the Greyhound worked her way through the green and picturesque archipelago of Boston harbour, the pilot did me the kindness of pointing out Fort Warren as my probable abode for some future months, and confidentially spitting in my ear the advice to "holler for the Union." He had also found occasion to essay some advice to "Jane," a negro woman, one of those tidy, respectable family servants, redolent of "Old Virginia," who had been captured on her way to join her mistress, the wife of a Confederate agent in Bermuda. Jane's response was not complimentary; for the experience of the Yankee, which that respectable coloured female had obtained from the amount of swearing and swilling on the Greyhound, had induced her to assert, with melancholy gravity, that "she had not seen a Christian since she left Petersburg."

The United States Marshal, who was introduced by the prize-master, with the whispered injunction that "we had better be polite," was a little Yankee with gimlet eyes, and who, with the fondness of his nation for official insignia, had adorned himself with a long-tailed coat, scrupulously blue, and garnished with immense metal buttons marked U. S. He was accompanied by three citizens, two of whom appeared to be civil and intelligent gentlemen, whose curiosity, if that was the motive of their visit, was subdued by their politeness. The third had an emasculated lisp, which I afterwards found to be characteristic of a certain class in Boston, and which was increased in this instance by the effect of the liquor he had drank. "He was a Virginian; he thought it right to indulge a little State pride." "Oh, to be sure," responded the prisoners, who thought the confidential injunction to be polite to the marshal included his toady. The fellow came up to me whispering something about "his sympathies being with Virginia, but it wouldn't do to let the d——d rascals know it." I was glad enough to repel the embraces of this creature without enquiring why it "wouldn't do" to testify his sympathies for Virginia, and how it was that his sympathies detained him in Boston, and kept him in the company of "d———d rascals." I afterwards discovered that he was a prize-lawyer, and preyed for a living upon Yankee crews.

The marshal having taken himself off with the prize-master, I was, about sundown, invited ashore by a severe-looking man, placed in a carriage and driven along the green skirt of Boston Common to a building, which I was told contained the marshal's office. That official had not arrived there, I was waved back into the carriage by the severe man. "Where are we going now?" I asked pleasantly. "*To the jail!*" replied the severe man, very sharply and sententiously. I protested that I was a passenger on board the Greyhound, already in communication with Lord Lyons, to protect my rights, as such, under the neutral flag on the high seas; and if the marshal or his deputy presumed to treat me as a criminal, and put me in a common jail, it would be at the peril of grave legal consequences.

The latter part of my protest seemed to affect the deputy, for he relaxed his brows, and had me driven to the Tremont House, where the marshal was to be found. I was readily released on my parole not to attempt to escape. At a subsequent hour of the night, having found my way to a very modest, but excellent hotel, where I registered as "E. A. Parkinson," from "New York," I, at last, relieved from the presence of authority, and the annoyance of impertinent curiosity, enjoyed the first undisturbed sleep I had had for many nights.

I was taking breakfast the next morning, when the negro waiter who attended me, surprised me by suddenly asking me, with a grin, "if I was not from the Southern country." It was useless to dispute a negro's intuition in this matter; and the poor fellow was so eager in his questions that I told him, without hesitation, where I was from, suppressing my name and my condition as a prisoner. He introduced himself as "Lew. Walker." He was the slave of some gentleman in Petersburg, and had deserted his master—or, as he described it in the polite Yankee vernacular, had "skedaddled" some months ago. He liked the North "tolerably well;" he had married in Boston, (I did not ask him the colour of his wife); but he said only a few of "his people" who had come North had been as fortunate as himself. "You see, sir, de change is too sudden for 'em," was his explanation. Lew. expressed a desire to return South, and said he would go right away, if he could get back without trouble. His desire in this respect was unpleasantly postponed;

as some weeks afterwards I read in the police report of a Boston paper, that Lew. had been caught putting a guest's portmonaie in the leg of his boot, and, instead of getting for it the traditional thirty-nine lashes in Petersburg or Richmond, had obtained a civilized sentence of six months in prison.

I felt something like translation to a new world in the gay streets and luxurious hotels of Boston. In the latter places, were to be seen knots of sleek, lust-dieted men, lounging and guzzling; in the streets, a dizzy show of well-dressed crowds, going to and fro on errands of business and pleasure, or in the idle excursions of ostentation. What a contrast to the scanty homes of Richmond, and its streets, where soldiers in dust-stained gray challenge the passenger, and where the eye has become accustomed to the home-spun garb, the mildewed uniform, and the other proud tokens of the unabashed and stern poverty of a country fighting for liberty! Oh, my countrymen! how my heart bounds to think of you, in the dainty and ostentatious crowd that besets me! Our tears, our dust-stained rags, our broken goods, our images of poverty—shall not history gather them into a monument more glorious and more enduring than any the hand of Opulence can rear.

I had been left to understand that owing to the delay of the Washington Government in attending to such small matters as the rights of liberty of individuals, I should probably have my parole for a week or ten days in Boston, and might enjoy myself accordingly. But what enjoyment! Wherever I ventured out, I was sure to get my dose of Yankee, and on all occasions of such "enjoyment," I was glad to get back to the privacy of the four walls of my little bedroom.

I might go into the parlours or the reading-rooms of the hotels, and see there the peculiar fungi of Yankee hotel society. I might sally into the streets, and see the equipages of "Shoddy," driven by solemn looking coachmen, dressed in black, with mutton whiskers. I might stroll into Boston Common, and be beset there by the itinerant Yankee with his "Respirometer," his "Grand Stereopticon of the War," or some other one-cent wonder. It is not strange that a plain Confederate might be disgusted with such a programme of entertainment. But I did find some amusement, at occasional hours, in walking through Washington street, and observing crowds of enthused Yankees, including strapping women, with strong minds and constitutional "yearnings," gathered around the garish lies of the newspaper bulletins, and devouring such intelligence as the "Capture of Richmond," "Rout of the Rebels," "Defeat of Hampton's Legion by Massachusetts Negroes," &c., &c.

There were two occasions in Boston which drew me from the retirement of my hotel. One was the celebration of the return of a Massachusetts regiment, from the lines in Virginia, their term of service having expired, and the "brave boys" having sought their homes in the very heat and crisis of Grant's memorable campaign. They had left Virginia at the very moment the great battle had been joined on the Rapidan. Such conduct would have been despised as an exhibition of selfishness or cowardice in the South, and a regiment of Confederates returning home under such circumstances, would have been hooted in the streets of Richmond. But the Yankee is too fond of "sensations" to analyze any moral question they may involve. The whole of Boston was in an uproar of delight to receive the returned regiment which was escorted through the streets with all the military display the city could muster: flags waving welcome; spreads of canvas in the streets entitled: "Honor to the Brave;" handkerchiefs and parasols flapped from windows; car-loads of school children; and a jam of omnibuses at each corner of the route of "the braves," crowned with admiring spectators. Then there was a dinner at Faneuil Hall, a speech from Governor Andrew, and complimentary honours enough to fill two or three columns of the next morning's papers.

Really, the most curious philosophy in the composition of the Yankee is his love of sensation: the most distinctive trait, too, of the nation, and one in such especial and striking contrast to the plain and serious manners of the Confederates. It has frequently occurred to me that an occasion of the sympathy of Englishmen with us in this war is the similarity of our manners, proceeding in each instance from the habit of a quiet and practical estimation of things at their right value. The Confederates are a people of habitual sobriety of sentiment, readily excited on due occasion, but much more so by the inspiration of abstract principles than by the names of persons. How different the Yankee! I have seen General Lee passing through the streets of Richmond without a huzza and without any other attestation of his presence than that of his being occasionally pointed out with a quiet and respectful regard. I certainly never heard of a mob of admirers at his hotel, or a deputation of Confederate damsels to kiss him, or poetasters reciting to him, in public, verses, or "masterly ballads."* But the Yankees must have their "big thing," and if there is nothing else to serve their appetites these people will actually exaggerate their own disgrace and caricature themselves rather than not have their "sensation" in the penny newspapers. We all recollect what magnified and gloating descriptions the Yankee journals gave us of the foot-race of their army from Bull Run to Washington—one of the first "sensations" of the war. And here we have a twenty-four hours "sensation" in Boston in the celebration of the return of a regiment of soldiers, who come home in the remarkable circumstance that they have not re-enlisted for the war, and have turned their backs upon their comrades at the brunt of the campaign.

The other occasion which took me into the streets was one of sad, memorable interest. I had seen in one of the city papers that two hundred Confederate prisoners were expected in Boston from the prisons in the West; they having taken the oath of allegiance and enlisted in the Yankee navy. I went to the depot to see these wretched men, and when I saw them filing through the dense crowd, with their emaciated faces and bowed heads, I could not find it in my heart to accuse them. There was the evidence in their pinched faces and flimsy rags of the devilish appliances of torture that had been used to break the spirit and impugn the honour of these unfortunates.

But in the behaviour of the crowd which received them at the depot there was a lesson which I trust I may never forget. The poor fellows were ridiculed at every step, laughed at, assailed with contemptuous remarks, and had to run the gauntlet of the wit of butcher boys and greasy loafers, well pleased with their supposed superiority to Southern "barbarians." Such was the *fraternal* reception of those who returned to Yankee allegiance. And in this scene of derision at the depot I saw in miniature what would be the real consequences of the return of the Confederates to the Union, and what meant for us the promised embrace of fraternal reconciliation.

Oh! my countrymen, death and the visitation of all other misfortunes and

---

* But what shall we say of the other most characteristic fashion of Yankee hero-worship—rewarding their military and naval commanders with sums of money! Thus, the New York *Herald*, of a certain date, says: "We are now about to make Farragut a present of one hundred thousand dollars, and Winslow a free gift of twenty-five thousand dollars. By-and-by we shall raise testimonial fortunes for Grant, Sherman and Thomas also." Daniel Webster in his lifetime did not hesitate to stoop to such gifts to his popularity; and the modern Yankee is certainly not an improvement upon him.

misery, rather than the embrace of our enemy! God spare us the pollution of contact with a people who have turned every thing to a lie, and who, ravening for our blood, smile and stab. Who could endure the triumph of the Yankee—the braggart exultation of the coxcombs of creation—the merciless dominion of the most cowardly and revengeful of mankind! Rather the grave cover us and our name, and our dear country pass away in the mist of blood and tears, than we should consent to this humiliation!

I had passed a week in Boston, entirely unknown and secluded, when an incident occurred that was to open to me a new and surprising interest in this Yankee metropolis. I was sauntering in the reading-room of the hotel one evening, when an amiable looking gentleman came up to me with a beaming face and whispered, "Are you not Mr. Pollard, from Richmond?" I was so taken aback by the plump question that I could not help answering "Yes." "I thought so," he replied quickly; "some detectives here know you; hush, talk low. I want you to let me bring a friend around to see you at nine o'clock this evening." I signified my assent, and awaited with some interest an interview about which there appeared to be some mystery.

At nine o'clock I received in my chamber the gentleman who had so unceremoniously introduced himself to me, and who was, indeed, to prove a friend, accompanied by a gentleman whose name was already familiar to me as one who had suffered for his early and brave sympathy with the Confederacy in this war. There are obvious reasons why I should not mention here the names of these friends and of other sympathetic persons in Boston, afterwards found, who surprised me, not only by the warmth and delicacy of their personal kindness, but by their sentiments for my country.

I sat up with my two visitors until near three o'clock in the morning in conversation on the war, answering their eager inquiries of men and things in the Confederacy. The next day it was insisted that I should be introduced to a number of persons in Boston who sympathized with the South; and some of my countrymen will be surprised to learn that to meet these persons I was carried to the Merchants' Exchange, to the offices of leading lawyers, and to some of the largest business establishments in Boston. I may say here that in the course of two or three days I met at least one hundred gentlemen in Boston, among its most influential classes, who expressed to me an ardent sympathy for the South in her struggle for constitutional liberty, and an earnest desire for the acknowledgment of her independence as the only possible termination of an unnatural and unhappy war.

To no one could this have been a greater surprise than myself. I had long been a skeptic as to the opposition to the Lincoln Government in the North, and had esteemed it nothing more than a demonstration of partizan machinery, in competition for office and power. But however correct may be this general estimate of parties in the North, what I was made a private witness of in Boston was sufficient to satisfy any candid mind that the Southern Confederacy had a party in the North of devoted and intelligent friends, however small in numbers, yet entitled to her consideration and gratitude. What was most remarkable was that these men sympathized with us not from infidelity to their own section, but on the high and intelligent grounds that the war involves the issue of their own liberties, and that the Southern Confederacy in this struggle represents what remains of constitutional law and conservatism in America, battling against a fanaticism which must at last be destructive of itself. A sympathy of this sort is valuable. There is, perhaps, other sympathy with us in the North proceeding from less honourable motives, the mere fruit of faction—properly entitled "Copperheadism"—which I am very much inclined to think is worthless and contemptible. "Sir," said a leading merchant of Boston to me, "I am not what is called a disloyal man. I want to see the South succeed because I want to see the constitutional issue she is fighting for succeed. I regard General Lee as fighting our battles as well as your own, and if he is whipped we shall have a despotism at Washington which will crush freedom in the North, as well as independence in the South."

In short, I had discovered a circle of "secessionists" in Boston, and had been cursing the black desert of heartless crowds before my eyes, without the least thought that it contained an oasis for the despised Confederate. I was overwhelmed with kindness by my newly found friends; offered a testimonial dinner which I peremptorily declined; invited to charming country places and suburban rides. Alas, from this amiable diversion my thoughts were to be soon turned into a channel of bitterness! What could avail even the most generous kindness of a few individuals when I had been marked as a victim by the Autocracy at Washington, and the iron wheel of its torture was being prepared to grind my life with such unutterable misery as the imagination of despotism could invent.

CHAPTER IV.

COMMITMENT TO FORT WARREN.—Horrours of the Yankee Bastile.—Torture of "A Brutal Villain."—A Letter to Secretary Welles.

I was taken from a sick bed to my granite prison and sack of straw. I had been suffering many months from nervous prostration; and so much had it been aggravated, by the anxieties of my situation, that I had taken myself to bed. I was lying there, the morning of Sunday, the 29th of May, when a deputy of the United States marshal entered my room, and ordered me to accompany him to Fort Warren. There was no explanation of this harsh and immediate summons, except that "orders had come to that effect from Washington." In vain I plead the confines of sickness, and sought the delay of a single day. "Could I see the marshal?" "No. The orders from Washington were to imprison me 'forthwith.'" "What was I accused of? Why was it that the other passengers on the Greyhound were so graciously liberated, and I alone sent to Fort Warren?" The officer did not know. So, without explanation, without notice, without process of any sort, I had been selected, the single victim, to suffer for the Greyhound, while her master was off for Canada, and the other passengers had been permitted, without a whisper of investigation, to proceed in the same direction. Perhaps my imprisonment, under these circumstances, was a complimentary distinction; but I must confess that, at the time, I could not, as the Yankees say, "see it."

In the beautiful Sabbath-day, full of sunshine, through the sparkling water, and along the green islands of the bay, I was carried to my prison-house, the sight of whose solid masonry, rising above the bright water, smote my heart with a strange agony. What mockery all this flashing and picturesque scenery of Boston bay, as I passed through it on the way to prison. Through it all I could see the horrid maw of the jail that awaited me, and the black veil that was to fall over my hopes, and drape them in mourning.

I was presented to Major Cabot, commandant of the fort, "registered," and was then asked to surrender my money and give an account of my effects. The latter proceedings were undertaken by Lieutenant Parry, the officer "in charge of prisoners," who dispensed with all that was unpleasant in them, and took my word that I had "neither weapons nor documents" in my baggage. This officer was very civil, and not only spared me the indignity of a search, but addressed me some polite common-places, kindly intended I thought, to compose my mind. He inquired when I had left Richmond; and asked with an appearance of great interest, after the condition of General Longstreet, who had been wounded before I had taken my departure from the Confederacy.

Here let me say, once for all, that I am satisfied the officers of Fort Warren showed, to the prisoners in their charge, all the kindness they could venture; but at the same time I am forced to declare that this disposition could do but little to mitigate that system of *punishment* of prisoners of war demanded at Washington.

I was consigned to a casemate, and a sack of straw for my bed.

As I passed the sally-port, in charge of a corporal, my name was called out, and one of a melancholy group of men advanced to meet me. It was V. of Richmond, but I scarcely recognized him, for his hair had turned gray, and his prison attire made him a strange spectacle. "You here!" I exclaimed; "how long have you been in this prison?" "*Eighteen months!*" was the solemn reply. I had never heard in Richmond of his arrest. But there were other terrible disclosures for me, which I had never heard in Richmond; which the people had never heard in Richmond; but which the Government in that Confederate city, had assuredly heard, and had kept to itself in silence and submission.

Kidnapped under a neutral flag, on the high seas; brought as human prize into the shambles of Boston; dragged from a sick bed into prison, when once I had passed through the sally-port of Fort Warren, I found a catalogue of misery that I never could have supposed to exist even in that most famous of Yankee bastiles.

Here in this fort, companions of my misfortune, were one hundred and sixty-odd men, the majority of them prisoners for more than a year. In a place facetiously called "the gun-boat," I found these men packed in three apartments, fifteen by sixteen feet.

Here, entombed *in solitary confinement*, were seven brave soldiers of the Confederacy, taken in Virginia and Tennessee.

Here, sentenced by a Yankee court-martial to *fifteen years* imprisonment, were two Confederate officers, Major Armesy and Lieutenant Davis; thus punished for recruiting Confederate troops in Western Virginia.

Here, in the quarters allotted to solitary imprisonment, brought here in double irons, was Captain Brattle, of Wheeler's cavalry, conveniently designated as a guerrilla, and treated as a felon.

Here I found *starvation* the uniform discipline of the prison; our rations these: one slice of bread for breakfast, one slice of bread and a morsel of pork for dinner, one slice of bread for supper—the slices so thin that one could almost see through them—these and a tin-cup of stinking cistern water comprising the entire bill of fare.

I did not learn these facts without a shudder. How long was I to continue here, and the words "*how long?*" seemed to reverberate in my heart like a knell. I was too sick to eat, and did not go to the cook-house, where, I was already informed, another horrour of my prison awaited me. I had learned enough for one day. As I laid upon my wretched bed at night, and watched the thin slice of moonlit sky, that shone through the grating, my nature seemed absorbed with unutterable horrour.

The hardships of a prison, its physical restraints, its beggar diet, are, after all, but slight evils, compared with the mental distress (aggravated, in my case, by a nervous constitution and diseased body), occasionally taking the form of a morbid agony, as the spirit wrestles for LIBERTY. For the first time in my life I felt the meaning of this precious word—no longer now the mere *decantatum* of poetry and sentiment. I had often used it as an idle ornament in language, but I little knew the sweet and hidden meanings of this noble word; how it signified the vital passion of man's nature, and contained the richest jewel of his inheritance from God.

I found in the morning newspapers the announcement of my incarceration, coupled with such comments as might be expected from the cowardly malignity of a Yankee, where its object is a helpless prisoner. The announcement in one paper was entitled "A Brutal Villain." Another administered the following warning:

"Some stronghold like that in which he has been placed is the safest quarters Pollard can find, as he is a doomed man among the surviving prisoners who have been released from Richmond."

But the following in a Pennsylvania paper (Pittsburg *Dispatch*) was a complimentary notice, especially to be preserved:

"To this man's course, unfeeling brutality our men attribute no small share of the indignities and hardships heaped upon them in Richmond, and his voice was never heard but against them

—never raised save to inculcate the justice or expediency of some newly devised brutality. He is one of that little band of malignants who have been engaged, heart and hand, for three years, in spreading among the ignorant masses of the South, the most villainous misrepresentations of the Government and the Northern people, and who have done more, as journalists, to sustain the rebel cause than regiments of soldiers in the field. For his exertions in this line, however, we could afford to trust him to the vengeance of the Government, but for his unwarranted and unmanly efforts to oppress the already overburdened prisoners in Richmond, we look to another source for punishment. Our townsman, Colonel Rose, and a score of others, well known and dear to us, have had a taste of this man's quality, and we ask for no other satisfaction than that chance may favour any one of them with a momentary meeting. There will assuredly be one educated villain less to labour in the rebel cause."

Of course, one's flesh might be expected to tingle at this foul and cowardly abuse. The next minute a sensible man would be inclined to laugh at it—especially the valiant threat of Colonel "Rose" and other flowers of Yankee chivalry. In another moment, reflection would teach him that he was complimented by such evidence of his personal importance, and decorated, as every true Confederate is, by the libel of a Yankee newspaper.

The sufferings I was to endure were to be terrible enough; but added to them was the constant smart of Yankee falsehood, which, ignoring the victims of its own cruelty, was incessantly publishing the imaginary misery of Federal prisoners in Richmond and elsewhere in the Confederacy. One can have an idea of the smart of this misrepresentation, if he will imagine a Confederate cut off from the world by the walls of a prison, and compelled to chew his indignation in silence, reading every day in Yankee newspapers some new version of "the barbarities of the rebels," and left to conjecture that the world is induced to believe these vile slanders, scattered to the ends of it, without the opportunity of any contradiction on the other side. But there is some possible comfort in the reflection, that Yankee falsehood in this war has overleaped itself. A people who, ravaging the country of their neighbours, burning their houses and property, and stripping the shelter over the heads of women and children, yet entitle their adversaries as *savages*, and assert themselves champions of civilization; who, fighting for the fourth year an unconquered country, have, in the entire history of that war, represented every event as a Yankee success, and a mortal blow to the Confederacy, are no more credible witnesses in these particulars than when they parade before the world their nursery dramas of the horrours of "rebel" prisons.

A few days before I left Richmond, I had had an accidental occasion to visit the Libby Prison, and was politely shown through all its apartments by Major

Turner, the superintendent. I little imagined then that I would have occasion soon to be instituting a comparison between my observations there and my experiences in the casemates of Fort Warren. I found the inmates of the former place, which has obtained such fearful notoriety in the North, somewhat restricted in space—the necessity of which restriction may be easily understood when it is known that there is such lack of house-room in Richmond, that every building in it is packed from cellar to garret, and entire families are often found to live in a single room; but the prisoners had comfortable bunks and long aisles stretching through the building, gave them the opportunity of exercise. These aisles were neatly swept by negro servants, who, broom in hand, were going through the building cleansing it, and thus relieving the prisoners of a disagreeable office. I learned that the prisoners were constantly receiving comforts and delicacies from the North; that they drew their pay regularly from the Washington Government; and that traffic in "greenbacks" being prohibited in Richmond, and it being necessary for the prisoners to convert their funds into Confederate money, our Government had, by a strained and punctilious generosity, put itself in the anomalous position of rating the enemy's currency in prisoners' hands at eight or ten times its own. I was struck by an abundance of pastimes in the Libby, that I was not prepared to see in a prison. Here were Northern newspapers and pictorials strewn around; cards, cribbage boards, dominoes, setts of games and other expedients to "kill time." The walls were garnished with sugar-cured hams, jars of pickles and delicacies long since forgotten in the homes of Richmond. I was amused to see prisoners sopping sweetmeats out of glass jars. I remember the remark I made on leaving the Libby and parting with Major Turner: I said to him that I had not been aware that there was so much luxury inside of Richmond.

I am not attempting extravagance, but fairly stating the results of personal observation, when I declare that I found many of the prisoners of the Libby living better in point of creature comforts, than some of our cabinet ministers in Richmond. Yet these men invariably go back to the North with stories of martyrdom in their mouths. A committee is appointed to make a report of their sufferings to Christendom. It gives a general invitation to those who will tell the hardest lies to indulge themselves without the fear of contradiction or cross-questions. It offers a premium for "raw-head and bloody-bones" stories, which may be told entirely at the pleasure of any liar or would-be-martyr, and with unlimited freedom in his vocation. It selects from sick prisoners returned to them, those consumed by fever or attenuated by chronic disease, bolsters them up on their beds, takes their photographs, and binds them in an official volume as the pictures of victims of "starvation" in Confederate dungeons.* Is it possible, indeed, that such flimsy devices of falsehood can impose upon the sympathies of the intelligent.

Thus the Committee on "rebel barbarities" prompts a witness from the Libby: "Were you not often very hungry?" "Hungry!" replies the witness, as if

---

* We have seen, as these pages are going through the press, an exposé in a Richmond paper of the cruel lie of the Yankee. It refers to an exchange of sick prisoners made in the fall of 1864:

"The mortality among our unfortunate prisoners sent by sea to Savannah to be exchanged was very remarkable. We have published a list of 117 who died on the passage to Savannah; also a list of 32 who died within a few days after being landed. Distressing as is this mortality, the Confederate newspapers have not been so inconsiderate as to impute it to a wrong cause.—Revolting at the shocking inhumanity which limits exchanges to the sick, the feeble and the dying, we have received home our brethren, emaciated as they are with long-protracted disease, and we have wondered not that so many died, but that so many, travelling in such a condition, should live.

"We have sent to the truce boat a similar class of the Federal prisoners in our hands; it is for these only that the Yankees have bargained. When the poor creatures reach them, worn and wasted by sickness, and evidencing, in their appearance, that they should be in the hospitals instead of travelling, in place of the sense of shame which the Yankee authorities and people should feel at the consequences of their inhuman policy, with such audacious hypocrisy as a Yankee only can manifest, they seize the occasion to calumniate the Confederates, a reluctant party to a commerce worse than "the middle passage," and only better than protracted imprisonment. They pretend to consider the returned men as samples of those who have been left behind; they charge their weakness and emaciation to starvation, and not to sickness; they clamor like so many howling dervishes; and with an effrontery that the world beside cannot equal, they extract self-glorification out of their own crime, and heap reproaches on us who are its victims!

"We know that their treatment of our prisoners is horrible enough. We know that of deliberate and systematic villainy, and without pretense of necessity, they torture the unfortunate soldiers who fall into their hands. We know, that in cool, fiendish calculation, they are kept in many of the prison houses under the torment of continual hunger. But much as we execrate such conduct, and the people who can practise it, we respect ourselves too much to slander them. We do not pretend that the sick men who are sent home to us are samples of the rest. We are not so false as to represent their emaciation as due to starvation and not to disease.—Multitudes of the poor sufferers die, as we have seen, on their way to our lines. Many die before we can take them to our arms. Many die before we can get them into our hospitals; and many there languish and die without a sight of the home for which they risked the travel. In all our distress at this mortality, we are candid enough to recognize the cause, and to tell the truth amid our resentments. Not so the Yankees. Their morals make it a merit to lie against their enemies, and so far from being restrained by self-respect, they are made zealous by self-felicitations. We trust the world understands them by this time."

that word was completely inadequate to his recollections. "Why, I tell you, some of our boys used to get things from home, and when they threw the bones into the spit-boxes, others of us used to be watching to pick them out and gnaw them over again."

The Committee is delighted; and the story of the scavenger goes to the Yankee newspapers as a tid-bit of Confederate atrocity.

To the sufferings of my first days in Fort Warren my memory reverts with an irrepressible shudder. If I had been in health I might easily have endured the hardships assigned me, including the straw sack, the diaphanous slices of bread and the bits of fat pork. But the nervous affection from which I had long suffered, and which was now aggravated by the anxieties and rude trials of imprisonment, had taken an alarming aspect. A partial paralysis of my body threatened to succeed. I could not rise from my bed or from a long sitting without finding my arm, or perhaps my whole side, temporarily powerless.

The kindness of my fellow-prisoners, in these circumstances, is never to be forgotten. I was relieved from my part of cooking and washing dishes, and was excused from "the police duty" assigned to prisoners, which included the cleansing of their quarters and a number of unpleasant tasks. My mess-mates came to my aid with friendly sympathy. I obtained medical advice from Dr Hambleton, of Georgia, my fellow-prisoner and excellent friend. Although I had but little faith in the justice or humanity of the Government at Washington, I thought it could scarcely insist upon torturing me, and would be satisfied to secure my person. I had applied for a parole on account of my health, but in vain had I waited for a reply. I had never, even, been allowed to see the order committing me to Fort Warren; and it seemed that the authorities had not been willing to spare me any agony of doubt or suspense.

I had been in prison nearly a fortnight, when I wrote the following letter to Washington:

FORT WARREN, BOSTON HARBOUR, June, 1864.

Mr. Gideon Welles, Secretary of the United States Navy:

Sir: On the 10th of last month, I was taken one hundred and fifty miles out at sea on a British vessel, where I was simply a citizen-passenger, unconnected with any public service of the Confederate States, and subject to none of the military penalties of your Government. Other passengers were released:

I, alone, of all the ship's company, an innocent passenger, was doomed to Fort Warren. I was taken from a sick bed to be brought here. In these harsh and invidious circumstances, I asked but a parole on account of desperate health: the bare concession of the plainest humanity. Since my confinement here, I have had an attack of partial paralysis. It is now only left for me to declare to your conscience and to the sympathy of the world—not in terms of importunity or any mere personal disrespect, but in the spirit of a solemn conviction—that I am being *murdered* by an imprisonment, the object of which is not to secure my person (since I offered to do this by an inviolable pledge of honour) but to punish an enfeebled body, and sharpen the torture of a disease that claims pity for its helplessness.

I am, etc.,   Edw'd A. Pollard.

To this letter I never received a word of reply or sign of heed. I was left to imagine the Yankee authorities chuckling with devilish satisfaction to know how their victim was pincered and excruciated with the tortures they had invented.

CHAPTER V.

JOURNAL NOTES IN PRISON.—Precious Tributes of Sympathy.—Portrait of the Yankee.—A New England Shepherd.—Sufferings and Reflections.—Fourth of July in Fort Warren.

June 17.—The hours weigh heavily upon me. In my imprisonment and sickness I have yet much to be thankful for, especially in the assiduous and cheerful attentions of my fellow-prisoner, Doctor Hambleton. The pastimes in our prison-life are meagre enough. Reading the newspapers and eviscerating Yankee falsehoods are our chief employments.

The good friends I have made in Boston have not forgotten me, and I have frequent occasion to acknowledge their kindness in missives of sympathy and occasionally of "material" comfort, in articles of food banished by "orders from Washington" from the slop-boards of our cook-house. Whatever thoughts I have of the cruel despotism at Washington and of those masses of population subject to it, my heart must always retain grateful and faithful memories of those few in a strange land who administered to my sorrow, and dared an expression of sympathy for me, when in the bonds of prison and disease.

I have a valued and interesting correspondence with some noble ladies in Boston, whom I have never seen, but whose names are known to several of the prisoners here, who have had various tokens of their sympathy. The correspondence in my case commenced with a present of delicious fruit, to which the card of the donor was attached. The charity of these ladies, and, more than all, the sentiments which have sweetened it, are treasured in the hearts of many prisoners here, and they may be sure that when the name and freedom of our beloved country shall no longer be disputed, their deeds will find a public record somewhere and be rewarded with conspicuous gratitude.

Before this war I had lived several years in Washington and in New York; but from all the herd of my acquaintance in the North I have not yet had one line of sympathy or of remembrance.

Yet I have had letters from *strangers*—among them dear, noble countrywomen of mine in the enemy's lines—which have touched my heart with inexpressible gratitude and pride.

I had been in prison but a few days when I received from Mrs. General ——, of Kentucky, a stranger to me, but the name of whose gallant husband, fallen on one of the bright fields of the war, lives in the glorious memories of the Confederacy, a letter of sympathy, subscribed, "a sincere though unknown friend." "Do you need aid?" wrote this generous lady. "And will you be allowed to receive any from your *friends?* It would be a pleasure to relieve your wants as far as we can."

Yesterday I received a letter which is so remarkable, that I cannot forbear transcribing here some passages from it, and taking the liberty of adding the name of the writer—a liberty, I think, which a grateful memoir must admit, unless there is good reason to the contrary:

PRAIRIEVILLE, PIKE COUNTY, MISSOURI,
June 12th, 1864.

Mr. Edward A. Pollard, (of Richmond, Va.):

I see from the papers that you are a prisoner of war at Fort Warren. All prisoners need the attention of their friends. Though entirely unknown to you, I have still the honour to be *a Virginian*, and love from a sense of duty all of her worthy sons. If you need money, clothes, or any thing, write immediately and inform me, with directions to whose care to send them. I have a holy veneration for my Mother State, and if I failed to do any thing in my power for her brave sons, I would feel that I had neglected a religious duty. All of my relatives, except my father's immediate family, are in the "Old Dominion." I have had a brother at Camp Chase, and a cousin at Johnson's Island, and have cause to know how comforting any sympathy is to the prisoner. Do not forget that you have many warm friends in Missouri, and in myself a faithful one. So do not fail to let me know if you wish any thing. I think, sir, that we partake of the independent spirit of our mother, and do not like to receive any thing from strangers; but you know Virginians are not strangers, but brothers and sisters wherever they are found....

KATE B. WOODROFF.

Sweet lady, God bless you! I wrote that I was in no such need as to tax the generosity of friends; that the letter of my fair correspondent was itself a treasure; that I was proud to have such a countrywoman. To think that she had written to a desolate prisoner thus from her distant home, with that hearty and persistent offer of assistance, so unlike cheap sympathy, so really anxious to oblige! Well may Virginia herself be proud of such a daughter! The fragrance of many a womanly deed breathes through the gorgeous wreath Virginia has entwined in this war, and among these we would place this tribute of filial love from distant Missouri.

June 18.—The following is an excellent picture of present Yankee society, which I came across to-day, in an odd book, which gave some account of France under the rule of Henry III.:

"There was no more truth, no more justice, no more mercy. To slander, to lie, to rob, to wench, to steal; all things are permitted save to do right and speak the truth."

What a perfect delineation of Washington and New York at the present day!

June 19.—The third Sabbath in my granite prison. Some one has had such care for the souls of Confederate prisoners as to have distributed among us a number of tracts, issued by the American Tract Society, 28 Cornhill, Boston. I have just finished reading one of them, entitled "Love Your Enemies"— a characteristic specimen of the Puritan Christianity of the Yankee, the blasphemy and *brag* of which have filled me with horrour and disgust.

The writer, evidently one of the pious spitfires of New England, sets out with a terrible denunciation of the Confederacy, and with characteristic regard for historical truth, describes the Confederates as outraging our [Yankee] "kindred," and "lurking in traitorous ambush at our [Yankee] door-posts." He then speaks of "their threats and curses, their outbursts of furious fiend-like passion." After this very Christian vituperation, and merciless vindication of the truth of history, our clerical friend encounters the question, how it is possible to pray that the wrath of the Lord be poured out upon the Confederates, and yet to retain Christian love for the *persons* of their rebellious neighbours. And he surmounts the difficulty bravely. The cause of the Yankee "*is the cause of God*," and to pray for the destruction of the enemies of the Yankee is "to divest themselves of all personal and merely human considerations" for God's glory, and to sink the love of the neighbour in the higher duties of the Divine service. This morsel of pious logic and Puritan charity is put in the following words:

"David recognized in his foes the foes of Jehovah and his church, and "planting himself by the very side of God, divinely inspired, he invoked the "most terrible calamities, the most complete ruin, even eternal evil, upon his ad-"versaries. Our cause, too, is the cause of God; our foes the opposers of those

"principles of eternal truth, justice, and righteousness, which sustain the divine
"administration. But do we stand, where David did, in unity with the divine
"mind and will, moved by the same pure and holy impulses, equally divested of
"all personal and merely human considerations? If so, then we, too, in calm,
"holy, fervent supplication, may pray, 'Render unto our neighbours sevenfold
"into their bosom the reproach wherewith they have reproached thee O Lord!'"

Has any one ever found anything more characteristic of New England Christianity than this passage—a mixture of old Puritan self-righteousness and modern lying, that might refresh the appetite of the Infernal! Concocted, probably, by some fellow who nurses his white dainty flesh with lace neckcloths, and spits pious venom in some fashionable church.

July 1.—I was allowed to-day to see a physician from Boston, who accompanied my sister, under a permit from General Dix.

This visit has been a precious occasion to me, and I trust, has improved my resolution to suffer with as little complaint as possible. Even imprisonment is not without its compensations and uses; is not necessarily a blank in one's life. We learn noble virtues in prison, for it is a severe school where we are taught to moderate our desires and to confront misfortunes with that defiant patience, which more than all constitutes the force of character and tests the man.

"To suffer, as to do, our strength is equal."

There is compensation, too, in the reflection that my imprisonment is in the name of my country, and that what I suffer is a sacrifice for it. It is true we all must contribute to the cause of our country in some form or other—and how little have I ever contributed to it, that I should begrudge this suffering in its name, and how many more deserving than myself, with mutilated limbs or broken hearts, have yet virtue to thank God that they have been able thus to testify their principles! These are salutary thoughts, which should chasten my pride and impatience, and teach me how little and unworthy I am, to resent the fortune which has made me a prisoner.

Fourth of July.—Captain Murden, of South Carolina, a fellow-prisoner, has celebrated the day by the following lines, entitled "The Confederate Oath," which we have all "taken." It is given as a specimen of the Fort Warren Muse, and as a sentiment appropriate to "the day we celebrate":

Aye, raise aloft that gory pall
  Of Freedom's bleeding corse,
While craven minions, shouting all,
  Its infamy indorse.
Gape, cannon, your infernal throats,
  Belch at the despot's word,
While Liberty's expiring notes
  Are in thine echoes heard.
Blow winds, from these accursed walls,
  And to the world proclaim
How wronged, insulted Freedom calls
  To stay the branding shame.
Tell of the rights our fathers claimed,
  And claiming, dared maintain,
Tell of the deeds in history famed,
  Which broke the tyrant's chain.
Then, tell again, how Avarice sapped
  The fane to Freedom reared:
How Lust, in false religion wrapped,
  To boasting minds appeared.
And let thy breath the poison bear
  Of Puritanic guile,
And in thy voice let nations hear
  The howlings of the vile.
Aye, hoist that foul, dishonoured flag,
  While truckling millions bow,
And kiss the rod, the chain, and gag,
  Upheld in terrour now.

And we, who see, and hear, and feel,
  That mockery of this day,
Shall WE, in servile cringing, kneel,
  And own the despot's sway?
No, by the rights our sires won,
  No, by the rights we claim,
No, while our wrathful blood may run,
  No, in our country's name,
No, by our fields of wasted grain,
  No, by our smoking walls,
No, by the Vandal-trodden plain,
  Our sack'd and ruined halls!
Bring from each corner of the land
  The demon's waste and wreck,

Bring murderous axe, and smoking brand,
　　The hateful pile to deck.
Then think upon the widow's wail,
　　Think of the maiden's tear,
Think of each wrong the Southern gale
　　Brings to your sickened ear:
Then by each stroke; then by each thrust
　　Which caused one anguished thrill;
Then by each deed of hate and lust,
　　Each heart-recorded ill:
Then swear while life's red current flows,
　　While flint can yield the spark,
While arm can nerve for vengeful blows,
　　Or bullet reach its mark,—
New England's lust, New England's greed,
　　Need seek no Southern sky;
While powder burns, or knife can bleed,
　　Who seeks our soil must die!

CHAPTER VI.

JOURNAL NOTES CONTINUED.—Life in the Casemates.—How the Yankees treat Foreigners.—Southern "Aristocracy."—Friends in Boston.—Massachusetts "Chivalry."—"Have we a Government?"

July 5.—We have quite a mixed lot of prisoners here. The officers and crews of the Atlanta and Tacony are confined here, and to Captain Webb of the first, and Lieutenant Reed of the latter, I am paticularly indebted for much entertainment and kindness. To tell the truth, it is not often you hear intelligent conversation among associates in a prison, or obtain any experience of small courtesies; selfishness, stupidity, vacancy of mind, are most frequently the results of the harsh and scanty life within the casemates, unless one should happen to have been bred a gentleman.

But I have been most fortunate in my mess, and I have yet to to notice any instance of bickering or of selfish overreaching among us. Yet we have plenty of pleasant controversy. My good friend Marrs (engineer of the ill-fated Cuba), keeps us all alive with his constant intention of "raising h—l": a vague threat which I have never yet seen him put into practical execution, for he really has an amiable and generous sentiment for everything but the Yankee. Captain Black reads the newspaper aloud every night, and Marrs punctuates with sententious exclamations. Then we have the invariable quarrel of each night about shutting windows and putting out the lights, two proceedings which always give rise to differences of opinion. Marrs must have everything read of the "d———d Yankees," or must have Captain Murden recite his composition of patriotic poetry for the day, before he can compose himself to sleep, which he at last does with objurgations not to be mentioned to ears polite.

July 6.—There are various devices here to induce prisoners to swallow the oath of Yankee allegiance. The most infamous is that practised upon the foreigners, who have been taken on privateers or running the blockade, and who through the offices of their consuls in New York and Boston, have been offered their release on condition of taking the Yankee oath of allegiance, and clinching it by enlistment in the Yankee army or navy.

In fact, there appear to be none of the rights of alienage recognized in Yankee jurisdiction. One must "holler" for the Union under all circumstances. In connection with these compulsory tests applied to foreigners, who are in the unfortunate category of blockade-runners, &c, I may supply the following paragraph, which I read some days ago in a letter from Washington, published in a New York paper:

"It appears that the rebel authorities again allow aliens to pass through their lines, as quite a large number of these refugees have reached this city within the past few days. To-day eighteen presented themselves at the provost-marshal's office, and took the oath of allegiance."

So, these men, whose neutral rights had been respected in the Confederacy, find, on reaching Washington, that it is necessary or convenient for them to take the Yankee oath of allegiance. It would seem, indeed, that the Yankees have assumed the task of annexing all nations to their political formulas, overriding all the predilections of foreigners and controlling the sympathies of the world. The arbiters of civilization, the bullies of all Christendom, the coxcombs of creation, they demand everything to give way as Mr. Lincoln "runs his machine" and dispenses the wisdom and bounty of "the best government the world ever saw."

July 7.—We had quite a discussion in our mess to-day. One of the company remarked that in South Carolina a mechanic was not respected as he should be. I took occasion to advance some peculiar opinions of my own: That the democracy at the North was an utterly false one, being an insolent assertion of equality, a sort of "d—n you, I am as good as you are," which placed two classes in society in an exasperated and bitter contest that was constantly going on in Yankeedom beneath the outward semblance of its social laws; that this insolent democracy was especially the product of free schools, that educated the population just to the point of irreverence and egotism; that in the South there was to be found the most perfect democracy in the world; that there was a voluntary and tacit acknowledgment of distinctions in Southern society (hence the conservatism of this part of America), and that, this difference once implied, the intercourse between the different classes was unrestricted and genial, with a pleasant admission of equality in all respects where equality was to be properly admitted. These propositions might be expanded into illustration and argument enough to make a book. But surely any one who knows anything of the South must have observed the easy and pleasant intercourse between its social classes, in which the humblest is treated with polite respect, so much in contrast to those insulting assumptions on the one hand and browbeating on the other, which make up Yankee society. Where a laboring man would, in the North, be stopped at the door of the rich by a servant, and held at arm's length in any intercourse the patron might find necessary with him, in the South, he could at least get a kind reception—certainly, would be treated with much more real respect than by the aristocratic Yankee with whom he contests the claim of equality a fraternity

---

July 8.—I have received to-day a gratifying letter from one of my lady friends in Boston She writes:

"Remember that you are to count us among your friends; and what is the use of friends, if you will not give them the privilege of ministering to you in prison. Send to us for anything you need. We are of the *practical* style, and our fingers and feet, as well as our heads and hearts, are at your service."

Such testimonies of sympathy illuminate the prison, and make us think more kindly of the world outside. God knows how my life in this Yankee Bastile was embittered with disease, and tortured by the cruelties of a government that denied me the commonest comforts. But mixed up with this wretched life our grateful remembrance of kindness unexpected and undeserved, which reached me, as far as it was able to defy the interdictions of official malice.*

---

* I may append here a peculiarly welcome letter from one of those ladies in Boston to whom I have referred—one, indeed, of the *practical* style, considering the gift which accompanied it.

My Dear Mr. Pollard:

I have great pleasure in sending to you a bottle of genuine Scotch whisky, which came from Rothesay, for us—the gift of a bonnie laddie, of whom we are very fond. Do you remember, some years ago, a very clever thing in Blackwood, called "Father Tom and the Pope?" In Father Tom's own words, I will only say—"if you'll just thry the full or a thimble ov it, and it doesn't rise the cockles o' your heart, why then my name isn't Tom Maguire." And by-the-by, I have a copy in pamphlet form of that same, which I will lend you. It will be *capital fun* for a hot day. Would you like it? This is really hot weather, is it not? To-day one would like to follow Sydney Smith's advice, to take off one's flesh and sit in one's bones. I hope you are getting better. Is there any chance of your getting a parole, and coming up to the city? It is bad enough to be among strangers, within prison walls, when one is well and strong. With all my heart, I sympathize with you, in your weary and depressing illness—away from home and friends. If there is any service we can render you, we shall be most happy to do so; and I beg that you will count us among your friends, and give us the privilege.

Yours, with warm regard.

July 14.—The Yankee newspapers we have got here, for several days past, have been in an incessant gabble about Early's and Breckinridge's invasion of Maryland. *Apropos,* here is a good "slap" at Massachusetts from a New York paper: "The Boston *Journal,* in a fit of heroics, wants to know how far an invading army of Confederates could march into Massachusetts. That would depend upon the time allowed the officials of that State to visit Kentucky and recruit."

July 15.—There is one question here constantly on the lips, or in the meditations of the prisoners. It is, "Have we a Government?" We do not hear of any thing done by the Richmond authorities in behalf of tens of thousands of Confederate prisoners, and we are left starkly and desperately to the contingencies of the future.

We know very well that it is not the fault of our Government that an exchange of prisoners is not made. Such an exchange has been estopped by the choice and action of the Yankees; and in doing so, this vile and sinister people have effected one of the most barbarous penalties of war—captivity. Such a penalty is opposed to the spirit and humanity of the age; in civilized war, the only object of taking prisoners is to exchange them, certainly not to condemn them to the savage horrours of captivity.

But, then, although our government is acquitted of the non-execution of the cartel, and this brutal infraction of civilized usage, why does it not manifest what concern it can for its prisoners, in some substantial acts of retaliation for the intolerable and terrible atrocities attendant on their imprisonment. This is where the question pinches. It is, with respect to outrages upon its prisoners that the Confederate Government has most abundant occasion and opportunity for retaliation; and it is with respect to this that it has done less to satisfy justice and vindicate the rights of belligerent.

There is a pitiable page of sophistry and weakness in the records of this war. It is the history of Jefferson Davis' policy of retaliation. While that history has afforded no instance of a single substantial act of retribution, it is replete with *pretences* of such, designed to conciliate the popular demand for retaliation, and to impose upon the world an appearance of spirit.

These pretences have been silly enough. Some days ago I read in the newspapers, that the authorities at Richmond had placed certain Yankee prisoners in a house in Charleston, in retaliation for the attempted bombardment of a city still inhabited by women and children. What nonsense! The peril of the prisoners is imaginary, when women and children walk the streets where they are placed without fear; yet it is a convenient text for the Yankee on the subject of "rebel barbarities," and an occasion, perhaps, for a prejudice against us, wherein we profit nothing.

The subject of Yankee prisons is theme enough for retaliation. There are in this fort, condemned to solitary confinement, certain Confederate prisoners, whose terrible doom calls loudly for the interposition of their Government, and illustrates how that Government has stultified itself by submission to the claims of the Yankee to enact the part of *magistrate* over those whom the fate of war has placed in their hands. I have been enabled to obtain some facts about these unhappy men.

CASE OF MAJOR ARMESY, &C.

Major Thomas D. Armesy was formerly a private in the Thirty-first Virginia regiment. He had raised a company in Western Virginia, near Clarksburg, and having turned this over to the Confederate service, went back in the spring of 1863, commissioned to raise a battalion in this part of Virginia. William F. Gordon, the adjutant of his old regiment, also took a part in this recruiting service, and was commissioned a captain in Armesy's battalion.

In April, 1863, Armesy, Gordon, and Lieutenant Harris, were captured by the Yankees in the houses where they were staying. They had taken the precaution to destroy their muster rolls, and to appoint a rendezvous for their recruits outside of the enemy's lines of occupation.

Armesy and Davis were taken to Fort Norfolk (near Norfolk, Va.), thence to Fortress Monroe, apparently for exchange; when they were suddenly ordered back to Fort McHenry in October, 1863.

They were tried by a Yankee court-martial. They were charged with recruiting in Western Virginia, a part of the Southern Confederacy, represented in its Congress, and, though overrun by the enemy, yet, legally, by the act of secession of the State, and by the express organization of our revolution, within the Confederate jurisdiction. There was but a single specification to the charge: *The official order of the War Department of the Confederate States, authorizing the recruiting service in which Armesy had been engaged.* On this charge and specification Armesy and Davis were sentenced to *fifteen years imprisonment at hard labour.*

A yet more terrible judgment was reserved for Gordon, who had also been confined at Fort McHenry. He was sentenced to be shot. On the day appointed for his execution in the fort, the brave Confederate had taken leave of his family, and had been marched out, carrying his shroud under his arm, with a dauntless air, when an order came from Washington, revoking the sentence.

The sentence of Armesy and Davis was executed by putting them to the dirtiest and vilest work in the fort, cleaning sinks, &c. They were subsequently transferred to Fort Delaware, and thence they were brought to this fort; their sentence being so far modified as to require them to serve out their term of fifteen years in *solitary confinement*.

MORE "FELONS" IN FORT WARREN.

I was requested by a fellow-prisoner in Fort Warren to communicate some facts in his case to the Confederate Government, and also to the authorities of the State of Virginia. David W. S. Knight was a member of the Twenty-fifth Virginia regiment, and on the 13th of August, 1862, was duly discharged from service. He then made his home in Stafford county. On the 17th of March, 1864, while pursuing his quiet avocations as a citizen of Virginia, a peaceable man in his own home, he was taken by the Yankees, and charged with the murder of one of their number, whom Knight had killed two years ago, when a Confederate soldier, and on picket duty as such. Knight had killed an enemy who approached his post, and attempted to overpower and capture him, and, in fact, was censured by his colonel for allowing an enemy to get so close to his picket line. He was treated by his captors as a felon, kept in close confinement in the Old Capitol prison as a murderer, and sent thence to Fort Warren, where he awaits whatever fate the enemy may assign him.

CHAPTER VII.

EPISODES IN PRISON.—A Council in the Casemates.—An Attempt to Escape.

July 16.—There has been a commotion in the prisoners' quarters in this fort to-day that so far exceeds the even routine of our days that it is entitled to a separate chapter, and, indeed, to a train of important reflection.

It appears that some days ago the Boston *Courier* had published a certain report that Major Cabot, the commandant here, had punished Confederate prisoners by compelling them to carry billets of wood on the ramparts. The report was untrue. It was contradicted by Major Cabot in the *Journal*. Thus the affair had passed out of mind when the following extraordinary publication, in the worst Abolition paper in Boston, fell upon us this morning like a bombshell:

FORT WARREN, July 13, 1864.

Major S. Cabot:

Dear Sir: We were truly mortified this evening on reading the Boston *Journal*, that you had been obliged to deny the slanderous attack—evidently intended upon your character—*this* being the *only* fort in Boston harbour wherein "Confederate prisoners" are confined.

We feel it not only a duty, but as an act of justice to yourself to deny emphatically the truthfulness of the communication which appeared in the *Courier* of yesterday, over the signature of W. J. F., purporting to be founded "upon the most ample authority." On the contrary, there are a very large number of "Confederate prisoners" who have been under your charge for more than *twelve* months, and we have always received at your hands nought but kindness and every attention and privilege consistent with the proper duties of your position. I have been requested by the prisoners to state that if you deem it necessary, you are at liberty to publish this letter.

In behalf of the prisoners under your charge, I have the honour to be, very respectfully, yours, &c.,

———— ————, Prisoner of War.

The fact was, that the prisoner who had composed for the Yankee press this compound of very objectionable grammar and gratuitous eulogy had done so on the responsibility of not more than *three* prisoners in the fort, the remaining hundred or so being entirely ignorant of this preparation of gratuitous incense to our jailours. I have suppressed the name of the authour of the communication, from a firm conviction, shared by all the prisoners with whom I have conversed, that he acted contrary to his better nature; that though thougtless, he was a faithful and zealous Confederate; and that he had been misled by interested advice into something worse than a *faux pas*.

The whole day has been one of excited criticism and sage council on this, our unexpected appearance, in Yankee prints. After much consultation, the subjoined letter was prepared for publication in a Boston paper, but was withheld from it, since the writer of the obnoxious piece agreed to disclaim publicly the authority he had assumed, to represent the prisoners in the fort (which he afterwards, I believe, did). While, therefore, it was not deemed necessary to publish in the Boston newspapers the following expression of opinion, yet the prisoners who signed it desired that it should be preserved and placed on appropriate record, as a testimony of their sense of propriety and duty in the general matter of the behaviour of prisoners. I have, therefore, introduced it here, with the names of its subscribers, as a record of Fort Warren that belongs to the Confederacy.

Fort Warren, Boston Harbour July 16, 1864.

To the Editor of the Boston Journal:

Sir: We, the undersigned, Confederate prisoners in Fort Warren, have noticed with great surprise, a statement addressed by ———— ————, prisoner, &c., to Major Cabot, and published by that officer in the *Journal*, stating " on behalf of the prisoners," &c., that "we," were "truly mortified" at a certain "slanderous attack" in the *Courier*, concerning that officer's treatment of prisoners, and proceeding, after these regrets, to contradict the same. In making this statement, Mr. ———— did not consult us; did not inform us; and does not represent us. We, therefore, request that you will grant us the same favour in your columns afforded to Major Cabot, to correct what you have published, and to say that we repudiate the statement Mr. ———— has assumed to make in our behalf. We do this because this statement refers to a matter entirely between Major Cabot and his accuser, with which we have nothing to do; because there is no occasion on our part for explanation—still less for sentiment—in a matter for which we are not responsible and with which we have nothing to do; and because—solely from our self-respect, without reference to the merits or demerits of the case in hand, without design either to cast an injurious reflection upon Major Cabot, or to bestow a eulogy upon him—we are so far sensible of the delicacy of our position as prisoners that we cannot see the propriety of our interfering as volunteers in a newspaper controversy, making ourselves the uncalled for panegyrists of any man, and putting ourselves unnecessarily and indecorously before an invidious public.

John W. Carey, c. s. n.	Edw'd A. Pollard.
J. Gillian King, c. s. n.	W. W. Austin.
T. L. Wragg, c. s. n.	W. McBlair, c. s. n.
James H. Hoggins.	J. A. Peters, c. s. n.
James J. Spear, c. s. a.	W. A. Webb, c. s. n.
A. L. Drayton, c. s. n.	Chas. W. Milburn.
James R. Milburn.	G. H. Arlidge, Lieut. c. s. n.
S. F. Marshall.	C. W. Read, Lt. c. s. n.
A. H. B., c. s. a.	W. B. Micon, Asst. Pay'r, c. s. n.
W. D. Archer, c. s. a.	E. H. Browne, c. s. n.
Chas. W. Delour, c. s. a.	J. A. G. Williamson, c. s. n.
D. W. S. Knight.	Jos. S. West, c. s. n.
James McLeod, c. s. a.	Thos. B. Travers, c. s. n.
Daniel Moore.	F. B. Beville, c. s. n.
Robert Hunt.	Thos. L. Hernandez.
A. Stewart.	John E. Billups, c. s. n.
Jos. M. Hertwood, c. s. n.	F. N. Bonneau, c. s. a.
James P. Hambleton, of Ga.	R. H. Gayle, c. s. n.
C. T. Jenkins, Fla.	J. M. Vernon.
Joseph Leach, New Orleans, La.	Thomas Marrs, Mobile, Ala.
E. O. Murden, Charleston, S. C.	Augustus P. Girard, Mobile, Ala.

The unpleasant occurrences of to-day have recalled some questions which have frequently been present to my mind, with respect to the proper behaviour of men who occupy the unfortunate, and in many senses, trying and delicate position of prisoners of war. It is certainly just and becoming that prisoners should recognize the kindness and courtesy of those who keep them; but this must be done in a proper way, and on a proper occasion, certainly not by the disgusting methods of a puff, or for the selfish and contemptible gain of the enemy's favour. Justice can be done even to an enemy, and it is only a base spirit that has recourse to falsehood and libel for its miserable revenge.

I think it is Rousseau, in his "Confessions," who tells of some person who, after breaking with a friend, went through the community, announcing: "Listen neither to this person nor myself, when speaking of each other; for we are no longer friends." The Frenchman exclaims this as magnanimous. Not so. A candid and honourable person can fulfil exactly and severely the truth to all men, and the confession that he and his enemy are equally disreputable in their statements, lowers him to the standard of that enemy, whatever it may be.

In these pages, I have made it a point to recognize whatever kindness has been shown me, although I have had no occasion to intrude such things into Yankee newspapers.

My own conception of the proper behaviour of one in the condition of a prisoner of war is, that he should consult the dignity of his country, keep aloof from all unnecessary conversation or contact with his enemy, and preserve a simple severity of manner, which, while guarding against any appearance of subserviency, equally avoids the imputation of an unmannerly insolence. For I have perceived that there are two extremes to be shunned in the behaviour of prisoners. One is toadyism. The other, and not less contemptible, is that braggadocio or swagger which affects to be patriotic spirit; but, in the condition of a prisoner, and under the protection which that affords, is really nothing more than a display of venturesome cowardice and native vulgarity. It is not necessary, for a prisoner to show his "Southern spirit," that he should quarrel with corporals and orderlies, and make insolent speeches to the officers who are put over him. Such a course invites insult and betrays the qualities which pocket it with indifference.

In medio tutissimus ibis. The prisoner of war must recognize himself as in the temporary power of his enemy, and make a becoming submission. But on the other hand, he must never omit to be sensible of the dignity of his country and himself, or forget to moderate his civility with the considerations of self-respect and propriety.

July 18.—We had in Fort Warren a very remarkable young prisoner, a boy, named McBlair, not more than fifteen years old, belonging to the crew of the ill-fated Atlanta. He certainly had a streak of romance in his composition, and Captain Webb, his commander, said that he noticed that the lad found an unfailing consolation in the casemates in reading *Monte Christo*, and devouring every book of adventure he could possibly obtain. The little fellow had often struck me by his modest and taciturn manner; but he had the spirit of a lion in him; and he has shown a fortitude I could scarcely have imagined in one of his years.

He made three attempts to escape. Once he had gained the parapet where one of the guards discovered him concealed behind a gun. At another time, he found in a nest of rags about the fort some old garments, in which he disguised himself, and boldly joining the gang of labourers who pass every evening out of the fort, had passed the sally-port, got down to the Boston boat, and had his foot on the plank, when one of the guards suspiciously noticing his fresh face, halted him, and carried him to headquarters. "So you were trying to escape, were you?" said Major Cabot. "I was doing my best, Sir," said the little fellow.

The third attempt of our persevering little friend was made a few nights ago, and came near proving a fearful romance. By feigning sickness, he had obtained admission into the hospital, and, as his only implements of escape had, by some mysterious management, secured a slight bed-cord and a life preserver. The night he chose for his attempt was dark, tempestuous, and as cold as some of our winter nights in Virginia. He had managed, by what must have been a difficult process, to squeeze through the narrow casement, and then had crawled up the parapet past the guard in the darkness and the rain. Still crawling along, he reached an angle of the fort, where he secured his slight cord to a gun, and fearlessly launched himself over a height of some twenty or thirty feet. The cord broke as he was descending, and he fell into the moat, injuring himself internally, and for some moments unable to move. His fall did not arouse the guards. He had now to crawl about one hundred yards past the sentries to reach the water's edge. Stunned, bruised and severely injured, he dragged his body in pain to the black and tempestuous water, over which he must have found it difficult to see even the shadow of the island a quarter of a mile off, where he might hope to get a boat and reach the mainland. Stripping himself to his shirt and drawers, and tying the clothes he had taken off to a plank, he adjusted his life-preserver, and boldly shoved off into the water. But the brave little adventurer had not calculated the temperature of the water; and, as he drifted off into the shadows, he found his wounded limbs benumbed, and his powers utterly failing him. Nature at last extorted from him the cry of a drowning sufferer. A boat was manned by the guards, and he was taken from the waters insensible. By the use of brandy and stimulants, he was enabled after some hours to speak. Major Cabot said that in consideration of his youth, he would overlook his effort to escape, if he would give his parole to make no further attempts. "No," said the brave and dauntless boy, "I'll try until I succeed." He knew the consequences of his resolution. He was put in a close cell, and doomed to that most trying of all tortures of the spirit, and which must, indeed, be maddening to one so young—*solitary imprisonment.*

CHAPTER VIII.

JOURNAL NOTES.—My Affair with Lord Lyons Ended.—The Niagara Falls Bubble.—Comforting Words.—How Dying Prisoners are Treated.

July 20.—I have ended my affair with Lord Lyons. I received to-day his reply to a letter I wrote him some days ago, and have rejoined; which, I suppose, concludes this vexatious correspondence. Copies of all three letters are annexed; and I shall spare myself any commentary upon them in my journal:

IN PRISON, AT FORT WARREN, BOSTON HARBOUR,
July 11, 1864.

Lord Lyons, Envoy Extraordinary, &c., for Her Britannic Majesty, near Washington, D. C.

My Lord: Will you please inform me what results have been reached, or proceedings taken, by Her Majesty's Government with reference to my application for release from this prison by virtue of the protection of the British flag, under which I was taken on the high seas.

I was brought here from a sick bed, at an hour's notice, and have been afflicted in my confinement with partial paralysis; and I am sure that this much said of the extremity of my situation will be sufficient to acquit me of importunity in again seeking at the hands of your Lordship a termination of my sufferings.

I have the honour, &c., your obedient servant,

EDWARD A. POLLARD.

BRITISH LEGATION,
WASHINGTON, D. C., July 17, 1864.

Sir: Your letter of the 11th instant reached me yesterday. In reply to the question which you ask, I have to inform you that I received yesterday afternoon the answer of Her Majesty's Government to the dispatches which I addressed to them on the subject of the capture of the Greyhound, and in which I enclosed copies of your letters to me.

The general instructions of Her Majesty's Government preclude my interfering, without special orders from them, in behalf of American citizens captured on board British vessels, seized for breach of blockade; and as Her Majesty's Government have not, on the present occasion, ordered me to interfere in your behalf, it is, of courrse, my duty to abstain from doing so.

I am, sir, your obedient servant,   LYONS.

Edward A. Pollard, Esq., Fort Warren, Boston.

FORT WARREN, BOSTON HARBOUR,
July 20, 1864.

Lord Lyons, Envoy Extraordinary for Her Britannic Majesty, near Washington, D. C.

My Lord: I thank you for your courtesy in replying to my different letters. I have, of course, no further claim to make upon it in that regard. But it is not improper that I should express a respectful dissent from the conclusion you have reached, and inform you that whenever released from prison I shall prefer to the Home Government of Her Majesty a formal claim for indemnity for a damaging and cruel imprisonment, to which I consider I have been subjected by the failure to obtain that protection under a neutral flag which was due to me under the law of nations and that of humanity.

I cannot concede, what is certainly a novel and inhuman doctrine in international law, that a *passenger* on a British vessel which has broken the blockade is so tainted in the breach of blockade that he may be taken *on the high seas*, under the neutral flag, as human prize by his enemy. If, as I am left to understand, my Lord, this is the position of your Government, it follows that it assents to a system of kidnapping under its flag on the high seas, and establishes against itself an astounding PRECEDENT. For if I, a passenger, was a legal prize on the Greyhound, then the British passenger in the same circumstances is equally so, being no more protected by the British flag on the high seas than I should be myself; and if, in these same circumstances, the Englishman does not share my fate, but is absolved by diplomatic intercession, this is the *favour* of the Yankee Government, which may at any time be withdrawn.

At one time your Lordship wrote me that you had requested my release. A another time, you write you cannot interfere in my behalf in any manner whatever. I am left to imagine that there is no other cause for this contradiction than that I am a citizen of a friendless and persecuted Government, towards which, yours, my Lord, professes neutrality, but, I must say, practices uniform disfavour.

Whenever restored to liberty I shall have full opportunity to testify to the damage of my imprisonment, as measure of the indemnity I shall claim from the British Government. But your Lordship will already perceive from the enclosed copy of my letter to the Secretary of the United States Navy, which has never been answered or noticed by him, that I have in vain entreated a parole on account of my health, in circumstances which appeal not only to sentiments of pity, but to the lowest senses of humanity.

I trust that your Lordship will find nothing in what I have written inconsistent with the high and courteous consideration due personally to yourself, or improper to be communicated, as I desire, to your Government in the interests of justice and humanity.

I have the honour, &c.,
Your obedient servant,
EDW'D A. POLLARD.

July 21.—It appears from Yankee newspapers which have got into the casemates, that there has been undertaken at Niagara Falls a peace negotiation after the style of Brandreth's Pills advertisements; in which Horace Greeley is intermediary of the Confederates, George N. Saunders, their fugleman—a flippant telegram of the latter to James Gordon Bennett, commencing the proceedings. It is to be hoped there is nothing in all this: that the Confederate Government has not for the *fourth time* in this war, when there is already a standing tender of peace and an abundant definition of its terms in the official acts and expressions of Congress and the Executive, sought the *back-door* of Washington, and put itself in a position to be snubbed and cuffed out of countenance by the master of the "White House." But we shall see how much of authority there is in these proceedings, and how much of the self-exhibition of notoriety-hunters and adventurers. In the mean time our little circle here entertains itself with the credulity of the Yankee newspapers, and their remarkable fecundity in making the wish father to the thought. An intelligent friend in

Boston writes me this evening, in dead earnest, "terms of peace are passing over the wires," and concludes with a flourish of piety and a fervent thanksgiving for the happy news.

July 22.—We were permitted for the first time this morning to walk a short distance on the island. I was touched to see the grave of a Confederate prisoner beneath the ramparts.

On our return to the casemates I found in the morning mail a comforting and sweet letter from my lady friend in Boston. I cannot forbear making an extract from it, as an evidence of the kind and Christian spirit of this excellent person:

. . . . "I can well understand all you must suffer of anxiety, and I sympathize most deeply with you. It is hard to bring one's reason and philosophy to the rescue, under circumstances of such peculiar trial. But, my dear friend, when these fail, faith comes in, and your heart will be lifted out of the depths, and comforted in the assurance that joy will surely come after a night of darkness and desolation. *In quietness and confidence shall be your strength;* and, if I ask you to trust, I am sure you will bear with me, and not think I am preaching to you. If I cared less, I would not say this to you. But it saddens me to know that you are suffering from a miserable feeling of illness and depression; and in my longing to do or say something to comfort you I may run—as women are apt to do—into what you would not be blamed for considering pious platitudes."

"I hope you will like and find readable 'Prescott's Life.' I have not read it yet, but promise myself that pleasure. If you will give the volume we send a place in your library, it will hereafter recall to you a passage in your life, which you may then not be entirely unwilling to remember. For this reason, I trust you will not consider it a burden, that I ask you not to return it. Remember if you think of *any thing* you would like, you are to write at once to No — for it. May God bless you, dear friend."

July 24.—Even the vilest criminal, at the point of death, is permitted to see his relatives, to communicate his last wishes, and to comfort his dying hour with the last embraces and tokens of affection.

A few days ago, Captain Bonneau, of South Carolina, a fellow prisoner, sick for many long months, was thought past hope of recovery, and the commandant of the prison was asked for permission for some person in Boston to see him. At any rate, Major Cabot found it proper to refer to his "orders from Washington," wherein it was stated that a prisoner in the last extremity of sickness might be permitted to see "his nearest relatives, IF LOYAL!"

The reader will ask, can it be possible that such an order can enter the brain and heart of man in this age of civilization and humanity! Can it be possible that loyalty to Abraham Lincoln, already made a test on women and children, and their right to breathe the air of their homes, is also to be made the test of the right to the last consolations of natural affection in the dying hour!—that the Yankee is to haggle about "oaths," and bring in his trumpery of temptation even at the grave!—that he is to whet his devilish appetite of torture in the last agonies of the death of his victim!

An unhappy Confederate might be dying and his wife be just outside the walls, come to him on the last errand of affection. She would not be permitted to see him unless she blackened her soul with perjury, renounced the country of her dying husband, and insulted the solemnity of death by coqueting with the politics of Abraham Lincoln.

One finds himself asking: is humanity stone dead in the Yankee heart, and has the world no conscience? Vengeance sleeps; but Divine justice has all the crimes of our enemies on its immortal record, and to doubt the day of retribution is to doubt the power of the Almighty.

CHAPTER IX.

JOURNAL NOTES CONTINUED.—A Yankee's Confession: Confederate Civilization.—A "Map of Busy Life" in Boston.— . . . Sickness and Reflections in Prison: Female Philosophy on the War.

July 25.—The Boston *Traveller* says: "It would only be as the vanquished that we could consent to Southern 'independence.' For observe what that 'independence' would mean. It would mean our abdication of the position of the American nation. Let but the Southern Confederacy be acknowledged by us, and it would succeed immediately to the place formerly held by the United States, in the estimation of the world. It would become the first power in North America, and if Maximilian should there succeed, Mexico would have the second place, while ours should be the third."

The Yankee is right. We Confederates are not only fighting in this war for independence, but for the front rank in the civilization of this continent, and for a destiny of power as well as of liberty. Such considerations ennoble the contest. Such prizes should stimulate our exertions.

But, apart from this reflection, there is an important truth involved in the declaration quoted above, which the Boston editor unconsciously admits and does not develope. It is that the South represents in this contest the better part of American civilization, represents superior ideas, represents what is most valuable in the traditions of the past, for it is only by such titles she could succeed "to the place formerly held by the United States."

And here opens an infinite field of interest to the intelligent inquirer. A comparison: on the one side, the North—its false and phosphorescent civilization—showy free schools, the nests of every social pestilence—material gauds—a society rotten with insolent agrarianism called "democracy;" on the other side, the South—its virtuous simpiicity—the extraordinary intelligence of a people educated, not so much by books, as by free institutions and by a peculiarly free interchange of mind between all classes of society—a popular innocence of mad reforms, "isms," morbid appetites, unnatural vices, and other products of New

England free schools—and, most conspicuous of all, a true and noble democracy; of which it may be said that, though the white labouring man of the South defers to those who are his superiours (not indeed in rights, but in the various particulars of society), no one more quickly or effectually than he resents the insult or contumely of power. Here are heads of reflection for a volume; and somebody should write it, to show the world how little it knows of the Confederacy, and how much it has been deluded by the lies, the boasts, the Thrasonical literature, and Puritanical pretence of the Yankee.

July 28.—

"What is it, but a map of busy life."—COWPER.

I have been interested to-day in a specimen of Yankee literature, "for the home circle;" the Boston *Saturday Evening Gazette*, an excellent specimen of that New England family literature which crops out in hebdomadals, illustrated papers, and other tokens of literary civilization.

With the usual amount of maudlin stories and poetry and reading matter for the home circle, the *Saturday Evening Gazette* furnishes its readers with a double-rate advertisement, in editorial type, on the terrours of Masturbation. This advertisement of a Boston quack is entitled an "essay," and placed in a conspicuous part of the paper, where it is impossible for the eye to avoid the nasty mess of literature and obscenity.

Let us look at the editorial columns. First we have the report of a sermon of a Boston clergyman, who edifies us with this discovery in the history and politics of America:

"The war of 1812 was an aggressive war, commenced in opposition to the wisdom of our best and wisest statesmen, to help Napoleon Bonaparte, the bulwark of despotism on the continent, and to destroy England, the last refuge in the whole world for the oppressed."

Following this instructive sermon are editorial "puffs" of various descriptions. A correspondent, whose palm has been evidently greased, gives the following glowing description of the attractions of a watering-place, which is evidently a candidate for public favour, with "its polite young lady waiters:"

"The tables at this house are filled with the choicest viands of the season, and being all short tables, each family may enjoy the benefits and pleasures of a full six-course dinner, as the ladies' ordinary, at three o'clock, is the dress dinner of the day, without being obliged to await the tedious formula of the long-table system. The attendants of the house are in the most part from your city, and we believe they are excellent selections, as the whole house has that air of sociability and contentment so peculiar to houses of its kind in the old Bay State. Hark! I hear the gong that reminds me that Putnam, with his host of polite young lady waiters, is ready to serve the ladies' ordinary, where I can witness the best-dressed ladies and enjoy an excellent dinner, all at the same time."

The *Gazette* is not sparing in its puffs. The reader is informed, in an editorial paragraph, of a certain person who cleans old clothes by steam. The editor vouches for him that "work will be done in that *astute* style for which he is renowned."

The reader's attention is next called to a camp-meeting in the vicinity of Boston. "These gatherings," says the seductive editor, "partake somewhat of the character of a picnic, and afford to many *almost the only recreation of the season*." Who would not visit this scene of New England piety, after such a recommendation, and the information that twenty-five cents will give him a passage on the "unrivalled" line of Blowhard & Co., to this pleasant Canaan!

Following the editorial matter, is an advertisement by the column of miraculous cures of almost every disease imaginable, invariably attested by the certificates of "clergymen." These medical advertisements are irrepressible, effulgent, and difficult to be epitomized. Here we have Cancer and Canker Syrup, Amboline (for the hair), White Pine Compound, Howard's Vegetable Syrup, "Ironized" Catawba Wine, Indian Emmenagogue, Cherokee Injection (with picture of big Indian), Dr. Wright's Regenerating Elixir, Hungarian Balsam, Chloasma, Pabulum Vitæ, Medical Hydrokonia, &c., &c.

A savoury list of quack compounds surely, with illustrative wood-cuts of women covered with hair by the use of "Amboline," etc., and regenerated skeletons "after taking" the nostrum, and all attested by the sacred testimony of clergymen, and other grateful, bedridden saints, who invariably send for the second bottle.

And, so with quack certificates; the card of an independent, wakeful clairvoyant; matrimonial brokerage; lewd advertisements of men and women for "agreeable companions;" and a few other specimens of filth, we have exhausted the delectable contents of the leading and model family paper of Boston. Is there not here a picture of coarse and purient life in which we may detect not a few of the characteristics and curses of New England "civilization?"

August 10.—I have written nothing in my journal for some days. In this time I have been sick, almost unto death, in these cruel walls. Tortured, too, from day to day, with every rumour and shadow of hope that flits through the prison, about the much-talked-of and long-deferred exchange of prisoners. From day to day I have carried the heavy burdens of sickness and disappointment; but though, at last, the strength of my body has rallied a little, the skill of the physician cannot so easily recover the mind. I can imagine a brutal submission to imprisonment, a sullen and coarse satisfaction in sleeping and dreaming away a life; but there are nervous, active sensibilities, to which a prison is more terrible than death—men who beat their souls against its walls and live in a frenzy of mad hopes. Alas for the fatal gift of excessive sensibility! Add to this a disease, which condemns one to the horrours of the bedridden in prison and fills the mind with gloom, and the circumstances excuse the most abject degrees of distress.

There was a little event of pleasant surprise in my life to-day. A box containing under-clothing, and, what was even better, something to eat, sent all the way *from the distant prairies of Missouri*, marked "from Kate W——." So it was from no strange angel, but from the dear Virginia lady who had written me before, and who would take no refusal of her kind disposition to serve me. I accepted the gift with a feeling of gratitude in my heart, which my pen could but very poorly express.

I have often had occasion to meditate, in this war, upon the abundant humanity it has shown in women. The fierceness of its strife has too frequently steeled the hearts of men, and demoralized much of our better nature; selfishness, mean expediencies, callousness, a certain carelessness for the misfortunes of others, since misfortune has become so common, have taken much of the place of the charities and courtesies of society. But in these, the worst ruins of war, our women, steadfast and conspicuous in their better nature, have not forgotten, even in the sorrows of their own hearth-stones, the claims of sympathy; but everywhere, in the hospital, in the prison, in every walk of charity, they have followed the impulses, and illustrated the duties of tender and unfailing humanity.

And then, too, how much superiour is woman's instinct in taking sides in such a war than the troubled reason of men. The women of Maryland and of Kentucky would give an overwhelming majority for the Confederacy; they, even while their husbands and brothers differ, are secessionists, almost without an exception; and even here, in the cities of the North, there are innumerable women who condole with the Confederacy, are in love with its virtues and sufferings, and dare expressions of sympathy and admiration in the face of prison, exile, and all the inhuman penalties which the Washington Government and its minions can proclaim.

There are some questions which require a certain complication of reason; others the key to which is found in a single direct and plain thought. Of these latter, women are the better judges. I have seen in a single paragraph in a woman's letter in a New York paper, the questions of this war more effectually disposed of than in all the sesquipedals of the editorial columns, and all the four years' arguments of the Yankee newspapers. "Men," says this female critic (she is talking of the male Yankee), "who would rather run than fight, any day, and who, if they are drafted, will hasten in abject terrour to the first emigrant ship which arrives, to secure a substitute, talk loudly about the glory of fighting and dying for one's flag and one's country. What is one's flag and one's country? It is not a strip of rag, or a little dirt, a few stones, and some water; these can be found anywhere, and demand no especial consideration. If our country and our flag are dear, it is because they represent to us a larger proportion of the blessings that make life desirable than can be found elsewhere. If these are forcibly taken away from us, if peace is gone, if liberty is gone, if friends are gone,—if home and plenty are gone, what is the country and the flag worth to me? All countries belong alike to God, and if a happy and peaceful life could be better secured on any other portion of this earth, that would become my country."

Thank God, we Confederates have a country to which we may claim a virtuous attachment, in which are wrapped up our individual welfare and our individual aspirations; in which we have pride and honour for the courage of its men, and for the benevolent missions of its laws to every home and fireside. Such a country a woman or child can love quite as intelligently as the man; for it is the expression of what makes life desirable, adorns it with unfailing objects of pride, and associates each member of the community, not notoriously unworthy, with the honours of familiar history.

CHAPTER X.

OUT OF PRISON.—My Parole.—My Boston Benefactress.—In Yankee Atmosphere.—A Letter from Boston.—Some Words on "Peace Negotiations!"—Waiting.

August 12.—A memorable day. For on this day after unspeakable and almost mortal sufferings, I was released from prison, on a parole, to remain with a relative in Brooklyn, until my special exchange, which I then supposed to be in negotiation, was completed. A concession obtained for me by friends, to whom my life-long, loving gratitude is ever due.

In the morning, Risk, the laconic orderly, came to my casemate with the short and severe message, "I was wanted at the Adjutant's office." I went there, and was told that I would be released on signing a "parole." The news upset my nerves, and brought my heart into my throat; but, alas! though liberated from the fort, I was yet to be confined in Yankee atmosphere. But I certainly was not disposed to quarrel with the partial favours of fortune, and so I signed my parole with a very lively satisfaction, and could hardly refrain from shouting for joy as I returned to the casemate to gather up my blanket and what few duds constituted my property in prison.

I was required to pledge my "sacred word of honour," "not to commit any hostile act against the Government of the United States, nor afford aid or comfort to the enemies thereof in any manner whatever, nor communicate to any one in the rebellious States, or proceeding thither, or to any one in Europe, or other foreign country, any information that may or can be used to the injury of the United States, and that I will report in writing to the Secretary of the Navy every two weeks, and hold myself prepared to return to Fort Warren whenever he shall so direct; it being understood that this parole is to cease at the pleasure of the Secretary of the Navy, or in the event of my recommitment to prison, or my exchange, or the termination of the war."

What a parting I have had with my poor fellow-prisoners—messages and entreaties for Richmond, good wishes, affectionate counsels, almost tears! Captain

Green gave me a ring of his own manufacture, and my good friend Marrs wanted to press upon me a gold chain, a remnant of property which the Yankees had, strangely enough, left the poor fellow. As I passed through the sally-port, I turned to wave my handkerchief to the weary, watching faces; but the sergeant orders me to "move on." I have left behind some friendships in those granite walls; and, if there, too, I have left a pleasant record of my companionship in the hearts of my unfortunate countrymen, God knows that I am prouder of it than of any other memory of my life.

August 15.—I was required to report in twenty-four hours in Brooklyn, but found time to see some friends in Boston. I saw my benefactress there, the noble Catholic lady, who had devoted herself to the comfort and consolation of the unhappy men in Fort Warren, and whose name should be inscribed in every record of honour in the Confederacy.

I shall never forget the brief time I spent in the delightful company of this lady and her family. The benevolent smile with which she met me, kindled my heart with a gratitude I could only stammer out in awkward words. But my awkwardness was brief, for in a few moments I felt at home—the feeling which is only the result of that simple grace and beaming sincerity with which so few can entertain a stranger. I remained several hours. There were tears in the eyes of this gentle lady when she read to me letters she had received from prisoners, and especially when she read a beautiful letter from a young Catholic priest, describing his feelings in visiting a field where some Confedrates had engaged the Yankee troops near Washington. He had found there the hat of a Confederate, torn and bloody, close up to the lines, and the incident he had woven into some touching reflections on the unknown gallant spirit that had met death, probably leading the forlorn hope of the day.

In that little family circle where I had suddenly stepped from the gray walls of prison, I found a solace and entertainment that seemed to impart again to me the pleasures of life. All were so kind and so interested.

The dear little girl who had actually bundled out of bed to see a "Southern prisoner," I had to tell of young McBlair's attempt to escape, and all our other little histories in the fort. Then she must show me her stock of photographs of the "poor prisoners," and with them some English caricatures of Lincoln, which, like all such specimens of English humour, were admirable, alike in portraiture and in point. I did not leave for my hotel until near midnight.

August 16.—I am yet strange and giddy in the comparative liberty of a parole after the horrour and torture of a Yankee prison. In the streets of Boston there was sounding in my ears the usual surly "halt" of some brass-harnessed Yankee at almost every step; and in the cars, whirled for twelve hours by the white houses and apple orchards of New England, and through the peaceful scenes of the country, I was imagining the reveille, the harsh call to the cookhouse, the orderly's round, and all the other routine of a day in prison.

I am living in a very remote suburb of Brooklyn; and here, *incog.*, and intent to avoid all social contact with the Yankee, I must possess my soul in patience, until, in God's good time and merciful providence, I shall again breathe the air of home and of liberty.

August 17.—A letter from my dear friend in Boston:

BOSTON, 1864.

I did not half tell you, my dear Mr. Pollard, how glad and grateful I am for your release. I did not realize it until after you had gone. The pleasure of seeing you face to face, of making you a veritable fact, after believing you somewhat a myth, of talking with you upon the one subject of deep interest to us both, was too much at the time to take in that other joy of your freedom. I suppose if I were a boy, I should have thrown up my cap, and made a noise like that "the shrouds make at sea, in a stiff tempest, as loud and to as many tunes." As it was, I followed the impulse of a womanly nature, and, kneeling down, I thanked Him who had heard our prayer, and loosed your chains, and opened wide your guarded prison doors.

. . . . We are getting up some things for the prisoners. What shall I put in for Mr. Pollard, was my first thought—forgetting, for the moment, that you had taken wings. I wish I had asked you more particularly what is best to send. I shall really be grateful for any suggestions. After all, *how little* one can do for so many. What are the five loaves and two small fishes among such a multitude. It is only that the doing one's best is acceptable from the sympathy it expresses. You, dear friend, entirely over-estimated the very little I found it a privilege to do for you. If I could atone by a life of service for the least of the wrongs my people (alas! that I should say *my* people) have inflicted upon as noble a race as God ever created, I should only be too happy. You must never think of any little thing I have done in any other way. If I have given you one moment's cheer or comfort, it has been more to me than to you that I have been able to do so.

I shatl hope to hear from you as soon as you have had your fill of sleeping between fresh, clean sheets. I think I would take it out after the fashion of Rip Van Winkle. And the pleasure, too, of sitting at a table with one's own friends, and eating in a Christian way! It must almost repay you for the hardship and keen discomfort of your prison life. No more rations, no more abominable pork. *Deo gratias!*

I have just received a call from a gentleman friend . . . . He is, indeed, a very true and faithful man; and the time will yet come when his voice will be heard above the wild waves of passionate strife, and his calm power will be felt. I intend writing him this week, and it will give me great pleasure to tell him what you said of him.

Well my friend, there is nothing else to write, but to say with all my heart, *God bless you*. And may He bring you to the haven where you would be, and give you the dearest desire of your heart and life everlasting. I know you will write me when you can. Say one farewell word when you leave, that I may follow you with thoughts and prayers of affection and true sympathy.

August 20.—Since I have been on parole, I have already discovered something of the public temper; so much so as to satisfy my mind that the great disappointment of the North, thus far in the results of the summer campaign of 1864, has given rise to a certain desire to end the war by negotiations. And it is not to be doubted that this desire has found some response in the South. The undignified and somewhat ridiculous overtures for peace made in this summer by parties, who, on each side, anxiously disclaimed that they had any authority from their governments, but, on each side, by a further curious coincidence, represented that they were acquainted with the wishes and views of their governments, cannot be altogether a story of egotistical adventures. They betray the incipiency, though an obscure one, of negotiations; and, I think, the times are rapidly making developments of the tendency of an appeal to compose the war.

I cannot anticipate what bribes may be offered the South to confederate again with the North. But one has been already suggested in the North: it is, to find an atrocious compensation for the war in a combined crusade against foreign nations.

The New York *Herald* declares: "With a restored Union, prosperity would once more bless the land. If any bad blood remained on either side, it would soon disappear, or be purged by a foreign war. With a combined veteran army of over a million of men, and a fleet more powerful than that of any European power, we could order France from Mexico, England from Canada, and Spain from Cuba, and enforce our orders if they were not obeyed. The American continent would then belong to Americans. The President at Washington would govern the New World, and the glorious dreams and prophecies of our forefathers would at length be realized."

To a proposition of such infamy of infamies, the attention of the civilized world should be called. What a commentary upon that European policy which has lavished so much of sympathy and material comfort upon the North, and, on the other hand, has rejected the cause of a people, who, as they are resolute in maintaining their own rights, are as equally, indeed expressly and emphatically, innocent of any designs on the right and welfare of others! The suggestion is, that of a huge and horrible Democracy, eager to prey upon the rights of others, and to repair by plunder and outrage the cost of its feuds and the waste of its vices.

The people of the Confederacy do not easily listen to suggestions of dishonour. Yet none are more open to the cunning persuasion which wears the disguise of virtuous remonstrance and friendly interest. It is here where the Yankee peacemaker is to be resisted and unmasked.

It will be for the Confederacy to stand firm in every political conjuncture, and to fortify itself against the blandishments and arts of a designing enemy. It will remember that enemy's warfare. It will remember that an army, whose *personnel* has been drawn from *all parties* in the North, has carried the war of the savage into their homes. It will remember how Yankees have smacked their lips over their carnage and the sufferings of their women and little ones. It will remember how New England clergymen have advised that "rebels," men, women and children, should be sunk beneath the Southern sod, and the soil "salted with Puritanical blood, to raise a new crop of men." To hate let us not reply with hate. We reply with the superiority of contempt, the resolution of pride, the scorn of defiance. Surely, rather than reunite with such a people; rather than cheat the war of "independence," and make its prize that cheap thing in American history—a paper guaranty; rather than cheat our dead of that for which they died; rather than entitle ourselves to the contempt of the world, the agonies of self-accusation, the reproof of the grave, the curses of posterity, the displeasure of the merciful God who has so long signified His providence in our endeavours, we are prepared to choose more suffering, more trials, even utter poverty and chains, and exile and death.

.... *September* 10.—The fall has set in, and yet no news of my exchange. I have written to Richmond of my failing health; but I fear it may be some time yet before I again see my brown South, and stand upon the "sacred soil" of Virginia.

Living here in seclusion—at least, choosing such severe isolation as I think becomes both the misfortune and resentment of a prisoner—consumed by anxiety, I have nothing left to sustain me but the promises of hope. And if I cannot hope successfully, I can at least hope bravely.

Anything rather than mere *nostalgia*, or that certain fatal charm of melancholy, which loses its misfortunes in idle sentimentalism.

He who learns to *wait* is more than all other men the master of his fortune.

CHAPTER XI.

PARTIES AND OPINIONS IN THE NORTH.—Vagabond Knights of Secessia.

November 17.—The great value of my parole has been the opportunities it has afforded me of immediate observation of the politics and society of the North, of introduction to many of their public men, and of a rare and extraordinary insight into the public spirit and real designs of the North with reference to the war. In these observations and studies I have been assisted by many verbal and written communications from candid and intelligent Northern men, who have freely exchanged their information and views for my impressions of Confederate affairs, which, indeed, I have been glad to give with emphasis on every proper occasion. The course of practical instruction afforded me in an interval of parole, in which I had free access to all quarters and classes of public opinion in the North, has brought my mind to certain distinct and firm conclusions, which, in certain respects, or, in some measure, have supplanted former theories of Yankee politics.

And of these, the first is that there is no considerable encouragement whatever to be found for the South in any existing party complication in the North, or in any element of conservatism there; that nothing remains for her but the arbitration of the sword, and the resolution of liberty or death. This is not a piece of rhetoric; nor is it an attempt at extravagance. It is a deliberate conclusion; formed against the natural desire of the mind to believe what is most agreeable; formed against my *first impressions*; formed after careful and unremitting inquiries in which I had the constant excitement of curiosity, the advantages of observation in the midst of the great political campaign in the North, and the assistance of an unrestrained personal intercourse with men of all parties and opinions, at the most important centres of thought in the enemy's country.

I had the opportunity of witnessing all the stages of public opinion in the North from August to November. When I came out of prison in the first-named month, the idea of "peace" was in active discussion; the Yankees were then discouraged at the failure of Grant, and the so-far negative campaign of Sherman. But then came successes for the enemy, and now the passions of the war blaze up more fiercely than ever. The people of the South should understand that all party changes in the North are constantly accommodating themselves to the course of military events, and that thus, on these events, the fortune of the South solely and severely relies.

Since the Chicago Convention, the Yankee peace party has moved inversely with the scale of military success, and as that has mounted in Northern opinion it has fallen, until it at last approaches zero.

No doubt can rest in history, that at the time of the Chicago Convention the Democratic party in the North had prepared a secret programme of operations, the final and inevitable conclusion of which was the acknowledgment of the independence of the Confederate States. It was proposed to get to this conclusion by distinct and successive steps, so as not to alarm too much the Union sentiment of the country. The first step was to be the proposition of the "Union as it was" in a Convention of the States; if that was voted down, then the proposition of a new principle of federation, limited to the foreign relations and to the revenue; if that was rejected, then the proposition of an *Inter-Confederate Union* to preserve, as far as possible, by an extraordinary league, the American prestige; and if all these propositions, intended as successive tests of the spirit of the South, were to fail, then at last the independence of the Confederate States, made the *sine qua non*, was to be conceded by the Democratic party of the North, as the last resort of pacification, and the one of two alternatives where their choice could no longer hesitate. It will be seen from this sketch of the programme that the design of the Democratic party was to get the North on the naked issue of war and separation.

The plan utterly failed in its execution. The fall of Atlanta gave a new lease to the war. And, aside from that event, it would have fallen through from the incoherence of the materials which, at that time, composed the Democratic party. In fact, the party, like all other Yankee minorities, went to pieces, and was swallowed up in the Presidential election, and may be said to have practically disappeared since then from the political arena, where, if it shows itself at all now, it is only in mock combat.

It was only necessary to observe the diorama of the Presidential campaign in that city of "immense sensations"—New York—to get directly before one's eyes the peculiar and unparalleled cowardice and subserviency of the Yankee in his parties and his political organizations. Some days before the election, New York was incandescent with revolution; processions flaunted banners and pasteboard through the streets, mottoed with what was, in the Washington definition, downright "treason;" the hotels and bar-rooms were choked with "secesh," vociferous, defiant, and generally half drunk. Yet, when Butler came, all this clamour and show left the stage as suddenly as one of Heller's spectacles, if not like it, in a flash of brimstone; and in one week's time, men, whose mouths had been filled with the fumes of revolution, and who had been breathing fire and slaughter, were as quiet as whipped curs, and not a whit more dangerous. Of course, the Yankee papers interpreted the exhibition of cowardly submission as the virtuous and magnanimous acquiescence in the will of the majority, a "triumph of republican institutions," and all that sort of nonsense; and what was actually the display of wretched time-serving of Yankee minorities, was put before the world by the effrontery of the New York *Herald*, and the ignorance of "Professor" Goldwin Smith as "the sublime spectacle" of patriotic self-negation and infinite moral virtue in Yankee politics.

I have asserted that there is little, very little, left of any "Peace party" in the North at the present time. It is necessary to distinguish the remnant of this organization from certain other sentiments in the North with which it has been frequently confounded.

Those people in the North who sympathize with the South, or affect any consideration for it, may be conveniently divided into three classes.

First, we may enumerate the so-called "War Democrats." They affect a great virtue on account of their opposition to Abraham Lincoln, but are quite ambidextrous on the question of peace; all they have ever said in favour of the termination of the war being nothing more than the whine of hypocrisy, as, from time to time, the military successes of the Confederates have extorted it. While playing their part against Abraham Lincoln, in which, in fact, they have no higher aim than partisan effect or public plunder, they attempt a popular compensation for this in pretending a virtuous attachment to a Constitutional Union, occasionally throwing into their opinions a little spice of blackguardism about "extreme men" in the Confederacy. These opinions are well exemplified in that infamous sheet the New York *World*, and that "nose of wax," McClellan. We will find the editor of this paper, one day, emptying his pot of filth on Mr. Lincoln, and the next day making a sort of popular amends and squaring his accounts with the vulgar, by low flings at the South, and a style of *double entendre*, that shows a wonderful proficiency in blackguard scholarship. The life of this party is equivocation. The writer was told that the editor of the *World* was at bottom a peace man, but had found it necessary for the influence of his paper, to use the pretence of "Constitutional Union" to catch the fools who believed in the possibility of any such thing: an example not only of Yankee newspaper morals, but a damning evidence of the incoherence and rottenness of the so-called Democratic party in the North, which finds such base equivocation necessary to sustain it.*

In the second class of Southern sympathizers, we may place that large number of persons in the North who persistently deny the right and policy of secession, but who feel for the people of the Confederacy, when they read of their poverty and sufferings, and think they have been too terribly punished for their errour. This sympathy is purely sentimental, and is quite worthless. It abounds in the parlours of New York. There are numbers of people in the North— ladies who have not unsexed themselves, and men who have not sold their sensibilities to the demons of faction—who are horrified and indignant at the cruelties of the war, and who pity our exiled women and houseless little children; but they will not admit the justice of the Confederate cause, and concede nothing to us but vague and fruitless commisseration. It is very easy to sit in a cushioned chair, with a full stomach, *and sympathize!* The South does not want such sentimentalisms. She asks for her justification in the eyes of God and man, and disdains a pity, that, denying it, offers a comfort that dishonours her. She will be content with no abridgement of her right. She has no claim on mawkish charities: no beggars' plea for the half pence and broken dishes of Northern philanthropy.

In the third place, we come to the "Peace party" proper in the North. It is composed of those who think that the war is essentially a crime and outrage:

---

*I am fully persuaded that a majority of the War Democracy in the North, are quite as much resolved upon the extirpation of Southern slavery in the war as the Black Republicans themselves; *although for different reasons*. They have nothing to do with the moral question of slavery; they disclaim all sentimentalism on the subject; but they think that slavery must be abolished by the war for State reasons, because it is an element of discord, and the Union cannot be firmly reconstructed without this necessary sacrifice to its future interests. They do not put this opinion openly before the public. Yet I have found it entertained by men who are even ranked as "Conservatives" in the North. The people of the Confederacy may assure themselves that there is a large majority in the North, without particular reference to the Black Republican organization, who are resolved on the abolition of slavery as the fruit and consequence of the war; and that such abolition is therefore the foregone and inevitable conclusion of submission, no matter under what circumstances, in what form, or to what master.

that amelioration of it will not do; that it is quite as much in the interest of the North as of the South to stop it; that the South represents in it not only her constitutional rights, but the traditions of the past and the whole cause of American liberty, and that in the defeat of the Confederate arms must go down the liberties of the North along with the independence of the South. Such intelligent sympathy is of real value to the South. But the party which goes so far is much weaker in numbers than is generally supposed by the Confederate people, and may be counted by hundreds, while the other classes, who all come, by a very violent connection, under the common catch-word of "Secesh," number thousands. It is especially represented by the New York *News:* a newspaper which is a marked exception to the rules of Yankee journalism in its decency and humanity of style, no less than in the real value of its arguments, and which may be taken as one undoubted, however small, example of Northern virtue in this war.

I must always remember for myself the kindness and encouragement I obtained from many members of this peace party proper of the North—those persons who held to their noble and simple faith despite political persecution, despite social ban, despite every injury and insult that could be offered them. Few they are; but let the South give them the full measure of their reward. I could not escape friends such as these. They invited me into their families, and in quite half a dozen places in Brooklyn (where I chose to reside in a hotel) I had constantly offered to me the privileges of a home, and could always obtain an unfailing and affectionate welcome. Again and again I have met persons who would say to me: "Can we do nothing for you? Do not hesitate to state any of your necessities. There is nothing too great or too small you may ask from your friends in the North." I had no occasion for myself, or opportunity for those of my countrymen less fortunate, to tax such friendship; but its cordial and persistent offers made none the less impression upon me.

But these people, it must be constantly remembered, are too small an element in Northern politics to demand, in that respect, much consideration. They constitute merely the skeleton of a party. There is so little virtue in public opinion in the North, so little that can be effected there by appeal to principle, that we must look for any considerable enlargement of the peace party in the North to the force of military successes, or the exhibition of undismayed endurance on the part of the South. We shall scarcely make converts or reclaim backsliders unless by such persuasion. It is the *military situation* from which the North takes its practical thought and purpose; and this which contains the only hope of the South.

While referring to party opinions in the North, I may extend the allusion to a certain ill-defined collection of people found in the bulk of Southern refugees and residents in the North. These people are very much abused in the New York newspapers, and deservedly so those of them who have preferred a cowardly ease in the enemy's country to the hard but honourable trials of war in their own. These derelict Confederates are the most contemptible of creatures. But it is only just to say that they do not broadly include all that much-reviled class of *Southern refugees* in the enemy's country. There are exceptions; some few and honourable men detained in the North by the confines of their domestic life, doing a good work, contributing to our prisoners, not noisy in their demonstrations, but holding their opinions decorously within the sanctity of their homes, or within the pale of the close society of those who think with them. But there are hundreds and thousands of these sympathetic absentees who, in a spirit of the sheerest cowardice and the grossest selfishness, exploit their Southern "patriotism" in the garish hotels of New York, and are trying to pass their time pleasantly among the creature comforts of Yankeedom, while the beloved people of the South are left to take for themselves all the privation and risk of the war. Many of them live extravagantly; not a few gamble in the Gold Rooms. And these refugees, dough-faced adventurers, fugitives from the conscription, and cowards of every stripe, who are bloating and pampering themselves in Yankeedom, talk "secesh" as loudly and bravely in the New York Hotel as in the Spottswood at Richmond. Despite the civilities the writer met in this former house, and its singular freedom from the pinchbeck of Yankee hotel life, he must remember occasions of disgust in seeing so many spruce "refugees" feasting, and wining, and guzzling in the delicate sops of New York luxury, talking Southern "patriotism" as fierce as baited bears, and in the next breath comparing their gains in cotton and the profits of their last mysterious trips to Nashville and New Orleans.

It is singular that this class are invariably the trumpeters of President Davis. They are so excessively patriotic that they worship him morning, day and night; they resent everything that does not represent the Confederacy in the colours of the rose; and every expression of Southern opinion, no matter what its manly and incontestable proofs of attachment to the Confederate cause, that implies a mistake on the part of President Davis, is fiercely denounced and forthwith tomahawked by these vagabond knights of Secessia.

The writer was informed that this peculiar Davis mania, at the expense of everybody else and every interest else in the Confederacy, prevails as much among the Confederate absentees and "sympathizers" in London and in Paris as in New York. This is not unaccountable, at least in good part. Many of these creatures are the agents and emissaries of President Davis, and, through his partiality, are reaping rich pecuniary reward in pretending to political adventures in the North and in Europe, and in flying certain financial kites for their own benefit. Thus the writer recollects to have met, in a company in New York, a little puddy gentleman, ruddy with good living, who could not be persuaded that Mr. Davis was not the "Moses" of Confederate deliverance. At parting, he hoped that the writer would recommend a certain financial scheme that a certain friend of his had gone to Richmond to lay before the authorities, by which millions of dollars were to be raised in Europe, after the approved fashion of extracting sunbeams from cucumbers.

The "sympathizers" the writer has described may well dread a party in the South sworn to uphold the standards of citizenship and society in the Confederacy; pledged to disown them when their tardy steps shall be turned towards our liberated country; and jealously resolved to preserve the fruits of our independence for those who have watered them with their blood, or brought them to their perfection by unwearied labour and sincere solicitude.

CHAPTER XII.

THE TRUE VALUE OF THE MILITARY SITUATION IN THE NORTH.—The Question of Endurance on the part of the Confederacy.

November 18.—An encouragement for the Confederate States in this war, of which our people have but little idea, is to be found in the true value of the military situation. The military successes of the North in the past campaign, and the glittering surface of prosperity in its borders, may incline the South to momentary fits of despondency, and to uncomfortable comparisons of resources; but when we come to reflect bravely and intelligently upon these, there are found causes of encouragement, which, although not obvious, are none the less real.

When a Confederate obtains the opportunity of observation in the North, and looks only at the surface of things, he is powerfully and painfully struck with the contrast they present to his scanty and war-ridden country. In some respects the contrast is appalling. He sees their large cities choked with a superabundance of able-bodied men; he visits military depots bursting with war material; he learns in Wall street that, despite the expenditures of the war, vast additions have been made to Yankee wealth, in the development of mineral resources, copper, iron and silver, along the whole slope of the Rocky Mountains; he is told that petroleum alone will, in a few years, be an article of export to the extent of one hundred and fifty millions of dollars, and that it has already founded—much more so than "codfish"—a distinct aristocracy in the North; he sees everywhere an almost riotous material plenty; he finds New York drunk with wealth and extravagance, every day vomiting into Broadway and the labyrinths of Central Park a dizzy stream of luxurious dissipation, and an endless procession of the triumphs of "Shoddy." The first impression of such a contrast, is that of immense endurance in the North, and the practical superiority of her war power in men, material and finances, over the military means of the South. That is the impression which generally comes back to us from flying visitors to the North, whose observations cannot be otherwise than hasty and superficial. Yet it is of all first impressions the one most thoroughly false.

The shock of contrast is soon over to the Confederate who remains in the North long enough to make a steady examination of the real spirit of the North in this war, and its relation to the apparent superabundance of resources in men and means. He gets a new light when he penetrates the surface of things; and if there is one truth which he discovers more plainly than any other in his observations in the North, it is that the resources, which at first struck him so strongly, are but to a little extent practically available for the purposes of the war.

It is necessary to come to facts to show this. It was my fortune to be in the North during the great exigency of recruiting their armies after Grant's butchery of the old Potomac veterans, and the immense expenditure of Yankee life in the summer's campaign. The system of Yankee recruiting was then, as I saw it, debased downright to the expedient of foreign enlistments and the arming of the negro. It is these means—scarcely anything more than these—which is recruiting the armies of the enemy. Their whole system of recruiting has passed to this wretched shift; and *beyond the short life of such a military expedient, the South has little or nothing to fear.* It is positively known that the Yankee armies are recruiting almost exclusively with negro troops; and information has been given me that at least three-fourths of the army of the James are composed of negro troops.

It is not asserting too much to say that the North must soon be practically more pinched for the want of arms-bearing men than is the Confederacy. The writer has not caught at loose assertions or idle rumours. The information comes from a general officer in the Yankee armies around Richmond, that the half-million draft yielded not more than seventy thousand *effective* soldiers. It was patched up with infamous frauds and absurd "commutations" to conciliate the opposition in the Presidential election of last November. In that election the vote of all the Yankee armies around Richmond was *eighteen thousand*, that being the proportion of native born and naturalized citizens of the United States in the combined hosts of Ulysses Grant and Benjamin Franklin Butler.

The difficulties of recruiting in the North are fast verging to the necessity of an actual conscription. To a great extent they must reach this dreaded and dire conclusion in the next call for men. It is only necessary to apply the invariable law of supply and demand to show what must be the difficulties in raising men, when we find bounties paid in New York exceeding one thousand dollars a head, the price of a single soldier. The bloated metropolis of the North may be able to afford such a largess. But in the rural districts, in the counties, and in the small corporations of the North, the system of bounties is already broken down. Counties in the State of New York have been designated to the writer which had already expended, each, about a million and a half dollars in buying human flesh; and others were named which had accumulated, on account of military bounties alone, a debt exceeding the sum total of taxable values within their jurisdiction.

It is under the pressure of the practical want of arms-bearing men, and in view of the fatal conclusion of an actual conscription, that the question has become uppermost in the Northern mind, how long the South can endure the necessities of the war. This simple question of *endurance* has entirely superseded all other methods of the solution of the war, all former questions of foreign interference, political revolutions, financial convulsions, &c.; and it is to all Northern men who discern the signs of the times, the one practical test that is to determine the destiny of the South. The writer is fully assured that all intelligent men of the North, including even leading Black Republicans who have not hesitated to confess themselves, are agreed that the North will never stand an actual conscription, and that if the war is pushed to that point by unflagging resolution, and unbroken endurance on the part of the South, it is just there that it will break down by the weight of an insufferable burden put upon one of the belligerents. The conclusion is not an extravagant one. In the South the conscription is doubtless imposed upon some few unwilling individuals; but in the North, with its inferiour motive in the war, and its peculiar character, it is utterly impossible to execute a conscription law upon a people who are wholly and absolutely opposed to it, who are not fighting under any doctrine of paramount necessity, and who have already given the most abundant proofs, that even the Yankee God of *money* is but little effective in enticing them to the battle-field.*

---

*The city of New York is scoured by "bounty agents;" yet even at this great centre of population in the North, these men find it necessary to their business to kidnap and drug recruits, and to entrap them by the most monstrous devices. Men are systematically made drunk to procure their consent to enlist; simple foreigners are put in "the Toombs," on false charges trumped up in emigrant boarding houses, and then persuaded that their only means of extrication is to go into the army; the drinking-houses, the gambling hells, the low boarding-houses on the wharves, every sink of iniquity, and every abode of ignorance, is constantly watched by the bounty agent for his victim. These practices are the occurrences of every day in New York. I happened to be cognizant of a recruiting affair, which took place in the hotel where I

It is almost impossible to describe the dread with which the Northern people contemplate the slightest possibility of a conscription. Even the draft of last summer, which only slightly threatened such a conclusion, was shunned as the plague. When it was thought that some of the ward quotas would be enforced in Baltimore, hundreds of persons left their homes and families there, fled for shelter to New York, and for months remained there in close concealment. It is well known that that city must be gingerly touched by the authorities of Lincoln; for it contains seventy thousand Irish, and, what is more, one hundred and fifty thousand people of the Catholic faith, who constitute in mass a pretty large seed of revolution, and who are considered to have made up their minds about the draft in the summer of 1863.

Observations which the writer made in the North, with ceaseless industry and under the stimulus of constant curiosity, filled his mind with the broad and strong conviction that never was the independence of the South more firmly assured than at this time, on the single condition that the spirit of the people and the army does not break by some unworthy impatience, or is not deliberately broken down by insane persistence in folly on the part of Davis and his clique of toadies and encouragers. A Northern conscription is the goal to which the South must press, and which already it closely approaches. A little endurance and it is won. It is the vital question to all intelligent persons in the North, how long our people will endure. They laugh at our expectations of political revolutions or financial rupture in the North; and they contend that the time is past when we may expect to win our independence by any grand military *coup*, or force of military successes. All these calculations are lightly or insolently regarded by Northern men. Their real anxiety is the measure of endurance on the part of the South. In a large intercourse with Northern politicians, the writer found that their great curiosity was as to the real spirit of the South, and the questions of thinking men among them invariably went to the point of the probable term of Southern endurance. He saw the value of this quality in Northern eyes. He became thoroughly convinced that by force of it alone the South would obtain her independence as sure as the sun would rise on the morrow;

---

resided in Brooklyn. Two men had picked up in Broadway an idiotic negro boy. They enticed him into the hotel, confined him in an upper room, and for a week plied the poor creature with confectionery, bon-bons and the best French brandy; until, at last, obtaining his consent to enlist, they stuffed him into a hack and drove him to the nearest recruiting office. They gave the negro one hundred dollars in small bills, and pocketed the balance of the bounty.—I may add that one of these parties was a Southern "refugee," and boasted of his exploit.

that such was the silent but general concession of the Northern mind; and that the future of the Confederate States was just at this time, and in the approaching exigency of a Northern conscription, brightened with a surer prospect of independence than any former situation of affairs had ever afforded.

There are two parties in the North, perhaps equally intelligent, and each claiming to draw their opinions from Southern sources of information, which differ as to the real spirit of the South: one claiming that it is resolute and even in the last necessity desperate; the other contending that it is fast being broken by reverses, and will end in submission. One finds this question in every circle in the North. Reliable information upon it is far more valuable to the Washington Government than maps of all the fortifications in the Confederate States. To convince the North of the spirit of the Southern people, is more important than half a dozen victories, for it is to convince them of the hopelessness of the war, and to put before their eyes the immediate necessity of conscription.

It is the simple lesson of resolution which the South must learn. It is the lesson for all events. When there is no occasion for hope, then make it the season of desperation; for this last quality is quite as good to dissuade the Yankee from the war as confidence itself. It will be easily inspired even in the worst extremity the future can possibly have, by a simple regard of the consequences of subjugation.

It is useless to expatiate, unless to those who are willfully blind, the theme of subjugation. If the spirit of desperate resolution has not already been drawn from what is known of the enemy's warfare, it will not be easily provoked by any other arguments. That spirit once fully demonstrated to the North, and the war is at an end. It is the only price of peace. There is not a scintilla of hope for the South in any political movement, or any peace negotiations in the North. It may be subjugation under a disguise, or subjugation by steps, but it is subjugation at last.

In view of the fate which threatens us in submission, and in view of the reward assured to us by simple perseverance, will the South falter? Will she who has endured so much fall away in a dastardly despair, and count all for naught, because, while she has strength, she yet has not resolution for what remains? Will she meanly break down in the last stretch of the course, when the prize and the sanctuary glitter before her eyes and the pursuing tread of mortal foe is behind her? History records the failure of many revolutions in their first stage: it is not often disgraced by the story of surrender because of the delay, and not the uncertainty of success. Surely there is no place in it for the repetition of this infrequent story at the hands of a people already ranked by former tests and endurances of this war among the most heroic of mankind.

CHAPTER XIII.

JOURNAL NOTES.—Letter from a Catholic Friend—An Evening Party in Brooklyn—Political Preaching—Renegade Virginians.

November 20.—I have received a letter from a Northern lady which is so full of sympathy and of generous Christian sentiment for my distressed country, that I have taken the pains to transcribe some passages from it in my journal. It is in reply to what I wrote, perhaps too gloomily, of my situation: my ears assailed by notes of Yankee triumph over late misfortunes of my country, and my heart filled with anxiety on account of the disappointment of my exchange:—

"It is hard—perhaps the hardest of hard things—to believe, to wait, to look up. The other day I was utterly disheartened about our cause. News came to us of grave reverses. One hope after another died out. And then white ashes lay cold and cheerless upon my heart. Then my good husband, who is always a comfort to me, brought the prayer-book, and read some of those verses so full of sympathy and so suggestive of faith and hope. So I, dear friend, would sit down by you and say to you words uttered by One who suffered. Listen: 'Take heed unto me and bear me: how I mourn and am vexed. They are minded to do me mischief, so maliciously are they set against me. My heart is disquieted within me; fearfulness and trembling are come upon me; my enemies are daily on hand to swallow me up. They daily mistake my words: all they imagine is to do me evil. They mark my steps when they lay wait for me; even mine own familiar friend whom I trusted hath laid great wait for me. *Nevertheless*, I have put my trust in God: I will not be afraid what man can do unto me. Be Thou my stronghold, whereunto I may always resort. Thou hast promised to help me, for Thou art my House of defence and my Castle.'

"It is sad indeed to think of the thousands who are lying in misery all over our land; and all the while deeper and wider flows the sea of blood. Ah, we need all that God can give us of grace and strength, or our human hearts would break. I would say human words of hope to you if I could. I have found how vain is the help of man. But, dear friend, an old, quaint writer has said: 'In Man's extremity is God's opportunity.' I wish you would write fully, unreservedly. I shall not wonder if you do not. It is much to ask you to take me wholly on faith. At any rate, unless you tell me that my letters annoy you, or subject you to inconvenience or suspicion, I shall write you under cover to ———.

"I got a letter from some of your poor friends sent on for exchange. They are lying within sight of the haven where they would be; but waiting and fearing every hour lest they be turned back to their prison. The trouble seems to be between Butler (I make the sign of the Cross in writing his name) and the War Department. I had hoped so earnestly that you would be speedily exchanged. What does it mean? Can anything be done? Write me fully about your delay and its causes. Who can tell what I might do? I have some influential friends who are so fortunate as to be—*black*. If I can make them of use to you, I will count it no dishonour to call them friends. I will make friends of the mammon of unrighteousness for your sake. Only tell me how the case stands—and trust me."

I was invited some nights ago, by an esteemed friend, in Brooklyn, to meet at his house, and take tea with a number of gentlemen who were in sympathy with the South, and interested to get all the information they could of Confederate affairs. I found at at an early hour in the evening some fifteen or twenty gentlemen assembled, among whom I believe there were only two of Southern birth. After the offices of hospitality had been abundantly performed by our excellent host, a "free talk" was at once opened among the company.

The conversation turned principally upon "peace movements." With reference to the negotiations at Niagara Falls, one of the company remarked that he had seen Mr. Holcombe, who avowed to him that he had been approached in this matter by Northern men, and that the suggestion of his part in the conference with Greeley had wholly arisen in this way. That is, I suppose, the simple Professor had been thimble-rigged, and was ashamed of the ridiculous part he had been made to play in amateur diplomacy.

I was asked as to the real design of Vice-President Stephens' mission in 1863. I explained that all the Confederate public knew of it was President Davis' published letter about the civilized code of war, &c.; although there was a suspicion, judging from the importance of the emissary, and the absurd futility of his going to Washington merely to protest against the enemy's cruelties in conducting the war, that he was secretly charged with a much more important and practical errand, which could scarcely have been less than to sound Lincoln on the question of peace.

A gentleman in the company remarked that he had it from credible authority (which he did not disclose) that Stephens was fully empowered, in certain contingencies, to propose peace; that the President of the Confederacy had sent him on this extraordinary visit to Washington, anticipating a great victory of Lee's army in Pennsylvania; that the real design of the mission was disconcerted by the fatal day of Gettysburg, which occurred when Mr. Stephens was near Fortress Monroe; and that it was in the insolent moments of this Yankee success that he was so sharply rebuffed by the Washington authorities.

This gentleman thought, considering the conjuncture of the occasion, that the President of the Confederacy, in seeking to signalize what he supposed would be a great victory of his arms, by a distinct and formal proposition of peace at Washington, had never occupied a prouder position, or one that better merited the applause of the Christian world.

I could not agree with him, and quoted, against such action of President Davis, his comparatively recent letter to Governour Vance, of North Carolina, on the futility and impropriety of essaying to open any special negotiations with the enemy on peace. There were the many distinct avowals of the purpose of the war on our side, in the declarations and acts of the Government, invariably protesting our simple desire "to be let alone," which were already a clear and standing tender of peace; the issues could not be made more distinct or more urgent than in the official record. Why should we go beyond it by attempts at kitchen conferences, which might not only be insolently rebuffed by the enemy, to the damage of our self-respect, but which, as our experiences had so far shown, were invariably misinterpreted, and not without plausibility, as signs of decadence and weakness in our military affairs.

Dr. ———— supported my part of the argument strongly. He thought the honour and self-respect of the Confederates had been lowered by these devious and unworthy attempts at peace. They were, of course, anxious for peace; but having once announced its terms sufficiently, they would do right, while awaiting the overture of the enemy, not to betray their anxiety, or open any unnecessary discussions of the subject. They could give no better evidence of their resolution than by such conduct.

By the way, Dr. ———— is the only one of the many "sympathizers" I have met in the North who has constantly warned me of the danger of over-estimating the value of this party, and, in fact, has decried their claim to any important consideration. He renewed this subject in the conversation to which I have referred. He insisted that the peace men in New York and Brooklyn represented but little wealth or social position, and that the influences combined in these advantages were almost exclusively ranged on the side of the war. I noticed that none of the company attempted to contradict this repeated declaration. And this, although all men, from individual pride if nothing else, are disposed to assert the importance of the party of which they are members.

There is published in the *Freeman's Journal*, of some recent date, a letter from Bishop Elder, (Roman Catholic), to the military commandant at Nashville, on the subject of the requisition of the authorities to have included in the litanies of the church prayers for Abraham Lincoln. I have never seen this subject so neatly and effectually disposed of as in a single paragraph of this letter. At first view, it might appear that the churches had made too much of this point; that to pray for the Yankee President might be enjoined as a duty of simple charity; and that to deny for him an act of devotion in which all men have a claim, was to make unchristian distinctions, and to raise unnecessary difficulties. A web of sophistry has certainly obscured this matter very much, even to honest minds. But Bishop Elder breaks this web with a stroke of his pen. In a few simple words he puts the question so fully and plainly that in his very statement of it he determines it, leaving neither necessity for argument nor room for dispute.

He writes: " The designating of an individual by his name, or by a special title, is not a part of my worship of God. And though if it would assist to excite devotion, it might be done innocently, and even laudably, when there would be no danger of its being misunderstood; yet to do it, *not for exciting feelings of devotion, but avowedly for the purpose of making profession of allegiance, and when it would be understood as acknowledging a right on the part of the secular powers, civil or military, to interfere in the arrangement of religious worship*—this would, to my mind, be a criminal betrayal of my sacred trust and a deep injury to the church, in which alone are my hopes of eternal salvation."

If there is anything more conspicuously infamous than another in the conduct of the Yankees in this war, it is their sweeping and proscriptive application of political tests: not only to all ages and sexes; not only to all human institutions of society, from the council and court to the district school; but, at last, to the churches themselves. The churches are required to pray for Abraham Lincoln; next to preach for Abraham Lincoln. The sequence is logical and unavoidable.

I have observed that it is already a test of orthodoxy in most of the churches of the North, that the decrees of Abraham Lincoln should be preached there as well as the word of God. Thus I read sometime ago in a Yankee newspaper, a communication complaining that the sermon of a certain distinguished preacher was a disappointment and an outrage, because "there was nothing to indicate that it was preached in the midst of a bloody rebellion;" "on word of thankfulness" for the emancipation of the negroes; "no Christian rejoicing," &c.

Where is all this to end? The habit of connecting politics with praying and preaching in the Yankee churches has already had the effect, by the unavoidable law of association, of breaking down the barriers of reverence. The effect of the association is, indeed, the most serious thing to be urged against the mania of political preaching; it is the direct occasion of irreverence; it introduces into the language of the pulpit the phrases of the hustings; and it must end at last in a blasphemy as prurient and disgusting as it is awful. Henry Ward Beecher, referring in one of his sermons to what he considered the hasty committal of the Democratic party at Chicago, to the hopelessness of the war, just before the tide of Northern successes set in to betray them, finds it necessary to explain himself by calling the Chicago Convention "GOD'S TRAP." One shudders at words to exceed which there is nothing in the vocabulary of blasphemy.

It was said recently by an English writer that there was no longer any vital christianity in the North. He might have added that even what was left of its forms, was fast being converted by the passions of this war into mere academics of politics—a class only a little more pretentious than the hustings and ward-rooms in the party education of the mob.

Among all the infamous monstrosities of the war, is there anything to compare with a Yankeefied Virginia woman! The misfortune of a marriage with a Yankee negrophilist is yet no reason that a Virginia woman should share the ferocity of the creature who is her husband, gloat over the sufferings of her blood and kindred, join in the cowardly twitters of Dutch-Yankee shopkeeping "aristocracy" about "barbarous rebels." Is it possible that the heart of a Virginia woman can thus divest itself, not only of all patriotic pride, but all generous sympathy and all natural instinct, forgetting, alike, the graves of the dead and the family altars of the living, to find, not an indifferent specacle, but an exulting prospect in the blood and tears of her own people! At what paltry price of sympathizing with a Yankee husband's fanaticism, and making herself agreeable to the company which surrounds her, is sold the birthright of a Virginian, and the natural affections of a life-time!

Priceless is that birthright. The man must, indeed, be lost to all feeling, and the woman worse, who does not feel a sentiment of pride that there courses in his or her veins the blood of Virginia—that historic blood, which has won the first honours in two revolutions, and whose golden track illuminates the records of this hemisphere. However obscure the life of the individual, there is pride to know that it is bound up in that of an immortal State, and that it shares, if by nothing more than the name of Virginia, the honours of history, the friendships of the virtuous, and the respect even of enemies. Who would barter this priceless inheritance for Northern wealth; the society of a nation of shop-keepers; the base creature-comforts of a vulgar luxury; the belly-timber and the upholstery of "Shoddy" aristocracy!

Not in insolent self-exultation, but with a profound sense of gratitude, and in deep humility, do I thank God that I am a Virginian. And to whatever obscurity fate consigns me, may I be known by my acquaintances to have worn that name, however humbly, at least not unworthily.

CHAPTER XIV.

A COMPARATIVE VIEW OF NORTHERN DESPOTISM.—The Record of Mr. Lincoln's Administration.

There are many persons to be found in the North, who admitting the rapid decline since the commencement of the war, of their government to despotism, attempt a consolation by the assertion that a similar lapse of liberty has taken place in the Confederate States. This opinion obtains, to a remarkable extent, even among those who are not unfriendly to the South, and certainly are not disposed to do her injustice. It must be largely ascribed to the very prevalent ignorance in the North, even among men otherwise well-informed and intelligent, of the internal policy of the Confederate States, and of the true spirit of their peculiar legislation with reference to the war. It is not only the Black Republican party that circulates the idea of an iron-handed tyranny in the Confederate States; but that idea is admitted to a large extent in the minds of those who are disposed to think well of the Southern experiment, but are not proof against the impressions derived from such peremptory laws as require men to take up arms in mass, to devote certain property to the government, and to hold themselves, generally, in subjection to the necessities of the war. These measures wear the appearance of the machinery of despotism to them; simply because they do not understand their true nature; while they add to their ignorance the mistake of viewing them from a stand-point which puts the North and the South in the same circumstances.

It is quite true that the conscription and impressment laws of the Confederacy are apparently harsh measures. Yet there is something to be said of them beyond the justification of necessity; and this is, that they are really nothing more than the organized expressions of the *popular devotion* of the South in the war; intended only to give effect and uniformity to it. They are not instances of violent legislation imposed upon the people; they are merely the formulas of willing and patriotic contribution of men and means to a war, in which not only a nation fights for its very existence, but each individual for the practical stake of his own fortune. It is difficult to make Northern men understand this: that, while they have a mortal terrour of the draft and other demands of the war, the people of the South are cheerfully willing to take up arms, and to devote their substance to the Government. It is thus that the conscription and impressment laws, which in the North would be the essence of despotism, are really in the South not edicts of violence, but mere conventionalisms of the war, through which the patriotism of the people acts with effect and regularity.

But beyond these laws, even the *appearance* of despotism stops in the Southern Confederacy. We have only to compare the established routine there with what we constantly observe in the North, to show how divergent, since the first gun was fired at Fort Sumter, have been the histories of the billigerents on all questions affecting political and civil liberty. There are no Military Governours in the Confederacy; there is no martial law there; there is, properly called, no political police there—our police establishment being limited to a mere detective force to apprehend, in the communities in which they are placed, spies and emissaries of the enemy. At no time in this war have soldiers ever been placed at a polling-place in the Confederacy; at no time have newspapers ever been suppressed; and at no time has a single instance of arbitrary arrest, or of imprisonment without distinct charges and the opportunity to reply, occurred within the Confederate jurisdiction. These are facts which carry their own comment on the base reflection, that in this war the South has declined along with the North in its civil administration, and has kept company with it on its road to despotism.

When we speak of the *despotism* at Washington, we do not design a figure or an exaggeration of rhetoric. We merely name a clearly defined species of human government, as we would any other fact in history. The Presidential election, just past, has given occasion for a full review of the acts of the Washington authorities. We may sum up that review in some brief paragraphs—dividing it into two branches: first, Mr. Lincoln's unconstitutional course on the rights of the States on the slavery question; second, his course on the rights of his own people in all matters of civil liberty—these two classes of outrage being a convenient division of his Administration, viewed both as to its intentions upon the South, and its effects upon the North.

I.

As to the Slavery question, it is only necessary to state the record.

1. The convention which nominated Abraham Lincoln President of the

United States in 1860, passed a resolution affirming "the maintenance inviolate of the rights of the States, and *especially the right of each State to order and control its own domestic institutions according to its own judgment exclusively.*

2. Mr. Lincoln in his inaugural of March, 1861, inserted this resolution at length, and declared that to him it would be "a law," and added, "I now reiterate these sentiments," and "in doing so, I only press upon the public attention the most *conclusive evidence of which the case is susceptible, that the property, peace, and security of no section are not to be in anywise endangered by the now incoming administration.*" In the same State paper he had before said, quoting approvingly from one of his own speeches, "I have no purpose directly or indirectly to interfere with the institution of slavery in the States where it now exists;" and subjoined, "*I believe I have no lawful right to do so; and I have no inclination to do so.*"

3. In Secretary Seward's famous letter to the minister of the United States, resident at Paris, designed as a diplomatic circular to the European courts, and written "by direction of the President," occurs the following paragraph: "The condition of slavery in the several States will remain just the same, whether it ["the rebellion"] succeeds or fails. The rights of the States, and the condition of every human being in them, will remain subject to exactly the same laws and forms of administration, whether the revolution shall succeed or or whether it shall fail. Their constitutions and laws and customs, habits and institutions, in either case, will remain the same. It is hardly necessary to add to this incontestable statement the further fact that the new President, as well as the citizens through whose suffrages he has come into the administration, has always repudiated all designs whatever, and wherever imputed to him and them of *disturbing the system of slavery as it is existing under the Constitution and laws.* The case, however, would not be fully presented were I to omit to say that any such effort on his part would be *unconstitutional,* and all his acts in that direction would be prevented by the judicial authorities, even though they were assented to by Congress and the people."

4. In his message to Congress of the 6th of March, 1862, known as his compensation message, after recommending to that body that they should pass a resolution that the United States ought to co-operate with the States by means of pecuniary aid in effecting the gradual abolition of slavery, Mr. Lincoln expressly disavowed for the Government any authority over the subject, except with State assent. His language was that his proposition "sets up no claim of a right by Federal authority to interfere with slavery within State limits, refer-

ing, as it does, the absolute control of the subject in each case to the State and its people immediately interested."

5. The act of Congress of the 6th of August, 1861, emancipated only the slaves of "rebels" employed in the "rebellion," and submitted the decision of such cases exclusively to the courts. Major-General Fremont, on the 30th of that month, he being then in command in Missouri, by proclamation declared free all the slaves within the State. This, as soon as it came to Mr. Lincoln's knowledge, he disapproved, and declared it in a formal order of 11th of September, to be void as far as it transcended the provisions of the act of Congress. And in a letter of Mr. Joseph Holt to President Lincoln, of the 22d of the month, that person being alarmed for the effect of Fremont's order, states that "the act of Congress was believed to embody the conservative policy of your administration." This statement Mr. Lincoln never denied.

6. On the 9th of May, 1862, Major-General Hunter, military commander of the department of the South, embracing Georgia, Florida, and South Carolina, by an order of that date, declared all slaves within such States free. On the 19th of the month, even before he was officially advised of the measure, Mr. Lincoln, by proclamation, declared the same, "whether genuine or false," to be "altogether void." In neither of these instances was there the slightest intimation of a change of opinion by Mr. Lincoln, either on the question of policy or of power. As to both, he then entertained the same opinion that he had announced in his inaugural.

7. On the 22d of July, 1862, Mr. Crittenden proposed, in the House of Representatives at Washington, a resolution which, after stating that the war was "forced upon the country by the disunionists" of the Southern States, declared that it "is not waged on our part in any spirit of oppression or for any purpose of conquest or subjugation, or purpose of overthrowing or interfering with the rights or the established institution of these States (the seceded), but to defend and maintain the supremacy of the Constitution and the rights of the several States unimpaired; and that as soon as these objects are accomplished the war ought to cease." In the House only two votes were cast against it, and in the Senate but one Republican vote, and it was at once and without hesitation approved by the President. No pretence was here suggested that slavery was to be abolished, or that any of the rights of the States in regard to it were to be interferred with.

Yet in the face of all this accumulation of precedents, we find *Emancipation* proclamations put forward under the claim of executive power—the first on the

22d of September, 1862, and the second on the first day of the succeeding year. In the last, all slavery in certain States, or parts of States, were declared free; it mattered not whether the territory or the slaves should fall within the military occupation of the United States or not. Such has been the sequel of a hypocrisy which must stand as a deception and outrage unparalleled in history.

But it has been said that the emancipation proclamation was a *military measure*, and to be justified as such from necessities outside of the Constitution. It is difficult to find patience to reply to such nonsense. The plea is the most absurd stuff that was ever put in the mouth of fool or knave to brazen out against the good sense and conscience of the world his fraud and outrage. Absurd, because we know, and all the world knows, that it was at the dictation and under the influence of a purely political party that the emancipation proclamation was issued by Mr. Lincoln. Absurd, because we know, and have had recent assurance from Mr. Lincoln himself, that he does not intend emancipation of the negro to end with the war, which it would do *ipso facto* if a mere military measure, but has made the abandonment or extirpation of slavery the preliminary condition for peace, and thus, therefore, a primary object of the war.

II.

It is this same dogma of "military necessity," applied to the slavery question, that Mr. Lincoln has used to fasten upon the necks of the white citizens of the North a yoke of intolerable despotism. It is only necessary to look upon what is every day passing before our eyes.

We see this despotism in the unreasonable searches and seizures of persons and papers, in direct violation of the Constitution.

We see it in arrests of obnoxious individuals and their imprisonment without warrant or charges preferred, and in some instances cut off from all communication with family, friends, or counsel.

We see it in the suppression of newspapers and wanton arrest of editors.

We see it in the assumption by the President of the power to regulate the right of suffrage in the States and establish minority and *aristocratic* governments under the pretext of guaranteeing *republican* governments.

These are not fancy sketches or the exaggerations of a narrative written with passion. We know that such things have occurred in Missouri, Indiana, West Virginia, Maryland, Delaware and New York; and yet even to question their legality is deemed disloyal, and men who maintain their inherited freedom in doing so, are designated by scurrilous abuse and threatened with the penalties of a despot's all-powerful displeasure.

To compare the falsehoods and crimes of Mr Lincoln's record with that rigour of measures in the Confederacy, which is really nothing more than the logical incident and the proper expression of resolute patriotism, is an outrage upon history. The noble memorials of self-sacrificing patriotism are very different from the scarlet record of ruthless despotism. The former adorn the South; the latter is forever the conspicuous heritage of Yankee infamy.

CHAPTER XV.

FROM NEW YORK TO FORTRESS MONROE.—Two Days in Baltimore.—A Bit of Romance.—Captain "Puffer."—The Negro Settlement at Fortress Monroe.

On the 28th of November, I received an order from the Navy Department in Washington, to report at Fortress Monroe, "with a view of being exchanged." I left New York that day. I had gone to General Dix's office to get transportation. It was with the greatest difficulty I could make my way through policemen and ceremonies, even to the honour of an interview with the *Assistant* Adjutant. There was a Cerberus even as far as the sidewalk: a very stiff policeman, who appeared to be a military mongrel, and who very insolently told me that I could not enter even the precincts of General Dix's headquarters without acquainting him (the policeman) with my business. This being done, and undergoing successive meditation, with a guard and an usher, I was at last permitted to see the least dignitary at headquarters—the Assistant Adjutant—a little bag-trousered Yankee, with an air of immense importance. He knew nothing about the transportation of prisoners, or did not want to know anything about it; and thought as I was travelling for my own advantage, no matter whether under Government orders or not, I must pay my own expenses! A pretty argument truly; but as it was no use to contend with impudence and a fool's brains, I yielded the point and took my departure. In ten hours I was in Baltimore.

I spent two days in Baltimore. I could not deny myself that pleasure; for I had many acquaintances and dear friends there.

It was refreshing to find here a difference of manners and dress, already bordering upon the quiet and simple tastes of the South. Not much of the glories of "Shoddy" here; no blazing ostentation and flippant affectations of vulgar wealth here; gentlemen plainly dressed, and ladies in decent, comfortable bonnets, not with little hats perked on the head, *a la militaire*, and swaggering a feather. The atmosphere of Southern manners yet lingers in Baltimore. But I was not to take my impressions from the surface, and I was anxious to learn something of the real spirit of this city, it having been so variously reported in Richmond.

Between New York and Baltimore there is a vast difference in Yankee rule. In the former city there is, properly speaking, not much of a "secession party," although plenty of a mere "Copperheadism," consulting purely partisan ends, and not at all dangerous. Hence there is no necessity for any special programme of despotism there; but in Baltimore there is a *real* secession party, and those who belong to it are kept in a partial condition of subjugation. Baltimore thrives, say the Northern papers; it is overrun and clattering with Yankee trade; but even in this gross prosperity the Southern sympathizer has no share. He is marked, he is degraded even in his business, all employment is closed to him, except such as he may choose to take as the subordinate or employee of the Yankee. All Southern men in Baltimore have found a discrimination in all trades and employments against them, and many of them have been compelled to retire from business. They tell you that life has become purposeless and intolerable to them. They have given up their business; they are pursued by spies; they are dogged by men who pick up their slightest word; they live in a constant atmosphere of suspicion. You look at these men and you see a blank dejection in their faces, a sort of melancholy devil-may-care expression. You never hear any eager or animated words from their lips; they have no appearance of interest in what they say; they seem to have drifted past hope; they look upon their future in blank dismay, or with the sullen indifference of men who have no longer any object to accomplish or ambition to serve, and who have converted life to a mere existence. And yet all this is but the faintest shadow of "subjugation," as it is designed for those now without the pale of the Union.

There is a striking difference between the men and women of Baltimore in their manifestations of Southern sympathy. It is painful to notice the careless manner and vacant air with which the first deliver their sentiments. But the women are very fierce and defiant, and talk vehemently about Yankee oppression and their attachment to the South. I met a number of them, who learned that I was on parole passing South, and were eager of the opportunity to send messages to their kinsmen and friends within the limits of the Confederacy. There was great excitement at the time, in the upper quarter of Charles street, on account of the case of Mrs. Hutchins, an estimable lady, who had been dragged from her family to a jail in Massachusetts, to be imprisoned five years, for having purchased a sword to send through the blockade to a relative in the Southern army. A deputation of some of the first ladies of Baltimore had gone on to Washington to get Mrs. Lincoln's intercession in the matter. But the lady of the White House had declined to see them, and had sent word from her apartments that "she could not see visitors, as she had her feet in a mustard bath."

It was said that Mrs. H. was required, in her captivity, to sew for Yankee soldiers. Others, in different prisons, were required to cook for them. "Oh, for such a chance," said one of the ladies whom I heard discussing these penalties of Yankee prisons, "wouldn't I cook for them with a vengeance—wouldn't I grind a black bottle into their soup!"

I was asked a great deal about our Generals and military heroes. General Beauregard appears to be the ladies' favourite in the North, and especially so in Baltimore. But I may say here that his reputation in this regard, or the reputation of any Confederate officer in any regard among Northern people, is nothing to compare with the unbounded admiration and respect in which General Lee is held by all parties in the enemy's country. I have heard Abolitionists utter all sorts of anathemas against men and things in the Confederacy, with this single exception: that I have never heard at any time or in any company in the North the name of General Lee coupled with a word of hate or of derision.

A few hours before I left Baltimore I received a hasty message from a friend, requesting me, by all means, to meet a lady who was anxiously waiting to see me in the parlour at Barnum's hotel. I repaired at once to the interview. I was no sooner introduced to the lady by our mutual friend, than, with agitated and plaintive words, she said she had learned I was proceeding to Richmond, and had come to entreat that I would make every endeavour to obtain the exchange of a certain Texas Colonel, who had been wounded at Gettysburg, had been a prisoner all the long months since, and was still confined at Johnson's Island. At the conclusion of her eloquent and passionate intercession, my friend playfully remarked that there was a bit of romance in the case. I had already guessed it.

This lovely lady, of gentlest type of beauty, living in a luxurious home in Baltimore, had left it to go to the terrible field of Gettysburg, to nurse the Confederate wounded left there. She did it faithfully; even the rudest of our poor blood-stained and dust-stained soldiers sharing in her gentlest ministrations. Among those who came under her care was the colonel of a Texas regiment; and then sympathy ripened into a more tender interest—and then it was the old, old story which I need not enlarge.

I vowed that I would make every endeavour to obtain the exchange and release of the officer. In fact, I resolved, if Col. Ould's "red tape" made it necessary, to apply to whatever authority there was in the Confederate States, capable of doing a knightly and generous act.

I arrived at Fortress Monroe on the brightest morning I had ever seen in winter—that of the 1st of December, 1864. I immediately reported to Col. Roberts, in command of the fort, who sent me to communicate in an adjoining casemate with one of Butler's staff officers, a sandy-haired youth who was still in bed at nine o'clock in the morning. But Capt. Puffer (a veritable name, not a *nomme de plume*, although I understood he was war correspondent of the New York *Times*) was, I must admit, very polite and gentlemanly. He said it would be necessary to communicate with General Butler, who was at the front; that, in the meantime, I might go on parole, but suggested that I should report my circumstances and status at the provost-marshal's office. The provost-marshal gave me another pleasant surprise of politeness. He indicated where I would find the hotel, and asked me if I was furnished with funds to pay the expenses of my detention. I may add here that this officer, afterwards, entirely at his own instance, refunded my hotel bill, and that I was, in all respects, treated by him with the consideration and civility due to a prisoner-of-war.

There is a good deal to see about Fortress Monroe, and I improved the comparative liberty of my parole there in such observations as I could properly make under its obligations.

One has an extraordinary opportunity here of testing the results of the Yankee dogma of negro emancipation and equality. General Butler has the merit in Northern eyes of having taken more pains with the negro, and having recognized his new status to a fuller extent than any other Yankee commander. So that observation of the condition of the freed negro in his department is made under circumstances of the greatest advantage to those who advocate emancipation, and insist upon its success.

Of the many thousand negroes, not soldiers, in the department of this General, the majority is concentrated immediately around Fortress Monroe. It is almost impossible to persuade them to remove to the North, as they have the strongest prejudice against a higher latitude, and cherish those local attachments peculiar to the negro, deriving a vague satisfaction from the thought that they are still on the soil of the South. Many of them express the greatest desire to remain in Virginia "after the war is over."

The point of land here is black with negroes. You see what one of Mr. Charles Reade's heroes describes as a "mixellaneous bilin' of darkies." You find the shivering old crones lining the beach with cake stands; negroes shuffling along the wharves hoping for somebody to give them a job; negroes thick as crows in the open lots around the fort; negroes poking their black heads through every open window for a mile around.

I had an opportunity of making an excursion through the whole negro settlement here. I had no sooner got into the Hygeia breakfast room than I was recognized by three or four black servants who had escaped from Richmond a few months ago, and had found employment at the hotel. They expressed boundless delight to see me; came up to shake hands; overwhelmed me with obsequious attentions, and crowded my plate with every delicacy in the larder. There were two Yankee chaplains sitting opposite me in undisguised and whispering amazement at such a demonstration of Virginia negroes to a "Reb," as they had no doubt been taught to suppose that such a character, in coming in contact with disenthralled Africans, was much more likely to have his throat cut than otherwise. All the negroes I have referred to had their budgets of experience to open to me. They were doing very well, as they were trained house servants; but "their people," "who hadn't larnt much," were doing very badly, and were "monstrous sorry" that they had come over to "de free side."

One meets here, but only occasionally, a fungus of negro gentility that is very amusing. I went out to the "Freedmen's Village" in a horse car. Seated opposite to me in the car was a fat-lipped mulatto woman, who had wonderful airs and graces. She languished; ogled one or two Yankee officers on the platform; was indignant because "dat man" (the white conductor) wanted to charge her extra for a band box, which she had placed beside her. I discovered from her conversation that she was employed as a sempstress in General Butler's family, and had just been out on a shopping excursion for herself through the stores on the wharf. "Sich mixed places," she said, addressing with a very patronizing air a coloured female, who was a shade darker, "dey ain't nice or 'spectable a bit; I gwine do my shoppin' in Baltimore next time." The "ginger-bread" female obsequiously wished to know if General Butler was made "Secerrerry of War," if her friend would deign to follow in his suite to Washington. "Oh, dear, no," was the reply; "can't leave de fort; and den you know—ha, ha, ha!—dese officers is sich sinners."

At the Freedmen's Village, and all along the road to it, there were invariable houses of scantling crowded with black people. I found several barracoons reeking with squalour, and with clusters of naked bodies of little black negroes hanging in the windows. Those wretched homes were stuffed with the meaner class of blacks, the poor "scrubs," who have no qualifications for sempstresses, barbers or waiters, and such "genteel" employments, and are content to pass their lives in animal riot and laziness, as long as the Yankee Government feeds them. What will they do after that? God only knows. Some of the more adventurous had built up quite a little outer town of "pie and cake" establishments—"pies and cakes"—nothing else, their enterprise had not got beyond that. There are hundreds of these establishments within a mile of Fortress Monroe. Many of these must have been open all day without taking in a copper. It was a melancholy pretence of doing something—those poor creatures sitting behind rows of stale and shrivelled pies, and waiting for impossible customers.

Alas! what must the future have in reserve for these wretched and helpless people! Some of them have already a dim dawning in their minds of the fate that awaits them. One notices that they are amused for a time by the surprise of freedom and the new scenes into which they are introduced; that they run after the drums and glitter of the Yankee soldiers; that, like children, they are excited and pleased by new spectacles, which are suddenly presented to them. But they soon relapse into blank helplessness.

CHAPTER XVI.

A DAY WITH GENERAL BUTLER.—The Civilization and Poetry of the "Sanitary Commission"—General Butler's Philosophy and "Little Stories."

Within thirty-six hours after reporting at Fortress Monroe a dispatch was received from General Butler, dated "Before Richmond," summoning me to his headquarters. I went up the river without any guard, being on parole. I had not passed up the James before for many years, and with melancholy interest, standing on the decks of the "River Queen," my eye traced along the banks the ravages of war. On the lower part of the river there were shrivelled spots on the bluffs where houses had formerly stood and where the destroyer had done his work; now nothing to be seen but naked chimneys pointing upward into the pale winter sky. I could see no signs of human habitations—nothing but here and there some squalid encampments peering over the banks, and soiled tents rocking in the winters' wind.

A gaunt man in a swaggy suit of black—a member of the "Army Sanitary Commission"—seemed very much inclined to enter into conversation with me. He had not the least idea he was talking to a "rebel"; he evidently imagined me to be an Englishman, judging my nationality, perhaps, from a round hat and red whiskers. I asked him what kind of people had formerly lived on the banks of the river. He proceeded to describe them, as he thought, for the benefit of a foreigner: very uncivilized; Vandals in agriculture, who wore out thousand acres of land to make as much in the way of profit as a Yankee could raise on a ten-acre farm; men who had been "raised with niggers" and were dirty "slouching" creatures, who had now made way for the pioneers of Yankee civilization. "Ah," he said, "you ought to see the banks of the Hudson by the side of this puddle. There's American civilization for you, Mister."

We were detained at City Point, which place I could hardly recognize. It looks so much like the wharves of New York, the river so choked with shipping, and the shore so covered with storehouses, that one might imagine himself here on the threshold of a great metropolis. I had to sleep on a hard bench on board the boat. A wretched night! Soldiers over my head singing camp songs and all sorts of dirty scraps of blackguard and blasphemy, alternated with sentimental ditties, furnished them by the Sanitary Commission! Think of a Yankee "scab," reeking with filth, a "bounty-jumper," perhaps, trolling out the verse which the sentimental writer of camp songs puts in the mouth of "the dying soldier"—

> "Soon with Angels I'll be marching—
> A crown of glory on my brow!"

The next morning, that of the 3d of December, dawned brightly through the forests of masts and mesh of transports into which the "River Queen" had inserted herself; and as the sun rose, we were moving up to Bermuda Hundred. Arrived there, I sought out the quartermaster's office, and was furnished with transportation in a comfortable ambulance to Gen. Butler's headquarters, about seven miles distant.

The road was not very good; but I had a charming ride in the bracing morning air, through a pretty forest of second growth of pine and oak. Before crossing the river on the pontoons the road ascends a table land on the south side, from which was spread out a lovely and picturesque scene in the hazy morning air, that alike ravished the senses and inspired the most vivid emotions of the heart. The high land stands in a bend of the James, thickly thronged with transports, tugs, men-of-war, with here and there a gloomy monitor; while above the banks floated the beautiful tri-color of the French frigate *Adonis*, a visitor to this scene of war. Stretching across the landscape, were the picturesque dioramas of a great army: tents gleaming in the woods; long lines of white-covered wagons toiling across the brown fields; horsemen flying hither and thither; human figures dotting the pontoon bridge; and now and then the train of some general's staff, in lustrous uniform, wending its way along the edges of the forest. I passed a file of nine or ten men with wounded arms or bandaged faces. "Them," said the driver of the ambulance, "is some of our boys what was in the fight last night with the rebs."

I reached Gen. Butler's headquarters about nine in the morning—a common frame building, probably an overseer's house, on the Aiken farm, flanked by rows of neatly constructed log cabins with brick chimneys and glass windows. I found at the door of the General's quarters two orderlies, one of whom required me to send in my "card" for the audience I solicited. Not being provided with the preliminary pasteboard, I substituted a dirty scrap of paper, and patiently awaited the General's pleasure to see me.

I had to wait several hours. At last the orderly called my name; and with a sudden effort I strung up my nerves for an interview with the man whom I had been accustomed to regard as the Raw-Head-and-Bloody-Bones of the war. After all, a surprise awaited me much greater than anything I could imagine. I had expected a storm of wrath to be exploded upon my head, without even the ceremony of salutation. Imagine my surprise when General Butler rose, saying very pleasantly, "Take a seat, Mr. P.," and then offering me a fragrant Havana, asking me "if I would not take what he could recommend as a very good cigar!" I excused myself from smoking, on the ground of "nerves." "Perhaps you would like to look over the Richmond morning papers; here they are, all five of them," said the General, sweeping a pile of newspapers towards me. "Ah, the *Examiner* is not there; *that* Gov. Bradford, who was just in to see me, would have."

The face of General Butler is familiar to the public in innumerable engravings, wood-cuts and photographs. But his large head and bust give one the idea of a bulky and unwieldy figure. On the contrary, he has a compact figure and a French quickness in his movements; he is short and well put up. His head is peaked with a forehead that slants rapidly, but just over his eyes shows a remarkable development of what phrenologists call "the organs of perception." He has small, muddy, cruel eyes; and there is a smothered glower in them, curtained in one of them by a drooping lid, which is very unpleasant. The other of his features are almost covered up in enormous chops, with little webs of red veins in them. But the expression of the face is by no means sluggish. He talks with a perpetual motion of his features, and has the Johnsonian puff in his conversation. When he essays to be pleasant he smiles; but as he performs this operation on one side of the mouth, and shows by it some bad projecting teeth, the effect is not re-assuring

After giving me time to make a cursory examination of the newspapers, General Butler opened the subject of my exchange. He said he was quite willing to send me through his lines to effect my exchange for Mr. Richardson, an attache of the New York *Tribune*, or whatever other equivalent was available; but in view of certain military movements on foot, it would not be prudent to do so at that time, and he would require me to remain inside of Fortress Monroe, until a proper opportunity to send me to Richmond should occur. He was polite enough to say that personally he was quite sure that I would honorably observe the conditions of my parole and give no improper information in Richmond with respect to what I might learn in passing through his lines; but he had to act in the matter with a view to his official responsibility, and under rules of military conduct which he could not dispense with. Of course nothing was left for me but to submit to the delay with as good a grace as possible.

Some officers being announced, General Butler requested me to withdraw, adding that he would see me again.

I had remained outside General Butler's quarters for some time, when a black servant obsequiously approached me with "the General's compliments, and would I, please, step in." Entering the room I found a table neatly laid for dinner, with silver service and snow-white napkins garnishing two plates. 'Mr. P.," said the General, "you will get no dinner unless you take some with me." If I had not been struck dumb by the invitation I would have answered him with more politeness. The General did the honours very graciously, and the bill of fare quite upset my notions of the diet of heroes: soup, roast beef and potatoes, apple sauce and other condiments, apple pie, cheese, almonds, and English walnuts. The table was attended by two negro waiters, whose appearance of cringing obsequiousness surpassed anything I had ever seen of such behaviour in the presence of a Southern master, and reminded one of the nervous awe which one might suppose the attendants and slaves of a potentate of the Orient might show in the august presence. I remember one of the negroes attempting to extricate for the General a cruet that had hung in the silver castor; and it was painful to see how his hands fluttered in the task.

After the cloth was removed, (I may remark parenthetically, there was "nothing to drink"), and the black servants had walked out on the tips of their toes, General Butler lit his Havanua, and launched into a long and entertaining talk. I must do him the justice to say that in this conversation he did not apply a single improper question to me, or, by the least allusion, offend the delicacy of my position as a prisoner. He did say, with an after-dinner yawn, "I wonder when this 'cruel war' will be over?" I ventured to reply that its termination was a wish common to both sides, and that I thought "it would be ended before very long." He must have discovered some implication in my reply, for he replied very fiercely, "I think so, sir; I think so, sir;"—and here military matters dropped.

General Butler talked freely of his own acts. He said that he had been much abused for two acts in New Orleans—the hanging of Mumford and the so-called "woman order." He had, as all men, some things to regret in his life; but these acts he could never regret; he hoped that when time had composed the passions of this war, justice would be done him, and that some of those who had abused him for his rule in New Orleans would find occasion to revise their judgments.

He said that when Mumford took the flag from the United States mint, he narrowly escaped drawing upon the city the fire of the fleet; and it was with great difficulty that the crews were restrained by their officers. The gunners on the Hartford had hold of the lanyards the moment they saw the flag taken down. He regretted the necessity of hanging Mumford. He (General B.) had received at least a hundred letters threatening his life if he dared to execute sentence upon Mumford; and when his life was begged by a very respectable citizen, but a few moments before he was taken to the gallows, he (General B.) replied that "in one hour it was to be decided whether he was to govern in New Orleans or not"—and he decided it by keeping the word he had first pronounced, and hanging Mumford.

As to the "woman-order," when Lord Palmerston denounced it, he might, if he had turned to the Ordinances of London, found that General Butler had borrowed it from that ancient and respectable authority. The "ladies" of New Orleans did not interfere with his troops; it was the demi-monde that troubled him. One of this class had spat in an officer's face. Another had planted herself vis-a-vis to an officer in the street, exclaiming, "La, here is a Yankee; don't he look like a monkey!" It became necessary to adopt an order that "would execute itself," and have these women treated as street-walkers. "How do you treat a street-walker," said General Butler; "you don't hug and kiss her in the street!" I professed ignorance. The General explained that he meant only that these women were to be treated with those signs of contempt and contumely usually bestowed upon street-walkers, so as to make them ashamed of themselves; and it was thus the order "executed itself."*

---

* I must not forget that, while on the subject of his rule in New Orleans, General Butler told me that there were some instances in which he did not require citizens to take the oath of allegiance, but was satisfied to accept their simple pledges of personal honour not to interfere with the authority he had established there. "But in such cases," he said, "I had to know my man: he had to be a man of undoubted personal honour with whom I thus dealt." He mentioned the case of a distinguished physician in New Orleans, who had said to him: "I cannot take your oath of allegiance; I would violate my conscience and affections to do so; it would be an act of perjury on my part, and one of deception towards you; yet I will pledge you my honour not to interfere with your authority, and, while it exists here, to employ myself only in my private concerns." "I admired his candour," said General Butler, "and did not insist upon any oath whatever."—Now whether this was a real occurrence or not, there is a lesson in it.

The General remarked that he had fed upwards of thirty thousand poor people in New Orleans. I replied, "I had no idea the bounty of his Government had been so extensive." "There was not a bit of *bounty* in it, sir," said the General laughing; "I taxed the people of New Orleans to reimburse every cent of it to the Government."

(N. B.—I did not think it necessary to say to the General that contributions of this sort was simply *Agrarianism*.)

The General said he had been doing the same thing in Norfolk and Portsmouth—feeding the poor. He sent his orderly for a copy of a newspaper—"The New Regime"—to show me the report of his Commissioners of the Poor in the two cities; by which it appeared that Government supplies had been issued to more than three thousand persons.

(N. B.—Done after the fashion of the New Orleans Agrarianism.)

Referring to affairs in Norfolk, I asked the General if he had ever come in contact there with an old acquaintance of mine whom I named. "No, sir," he replied; "but your question reminds me of 'a little story.' A professor of one of our colleges was at a dinner party, when one of the gentlemen present asked how his son was getting along at college. The professor replied he was not aware he had a son in the college. The parental pride was of course a little wounded at this ignoring of his Young Hopeful. 'You musn't be concerned,'

I am fully persuaded that it is the course of candour, self-respect and dignity that obtains even from such an enemy as the Yankee, a better treatment than any acts of self-abasement. The men who do these last are ground into the dust. Those who easily take the oath of allegiance purchase it by infamy, suspicion and surveillance. This has been my invariable observation in the North. 'A Yankee officer at Fortress Monroe told me that he did not believe "a Southern *gentleman* ever took the oath of allegiance." This oath is a livery of dishonour, with which the Yankee attempts a wanton debasement of his victim. It has no other value in his eyes. It can never obtain that consideration from the enemy which candid manners and erect dignity, and the proud assertion of one's personal honour never fail to win even from the meanest of mankind.

One of the worst Abolition editors in New York asked a friend of mine, if I could not be persuaded to take the oath of allegiance. My friend replied that, "he would answer with his and my life that I would never thus debase myself." "Well," said this blackest of Black Republican editors, "he is right; he couldn't do it without a contradiction of himself, in which nobody would believe."

Let the man who has the oath of allegiance pressed upon him, simply defy it. The design of the oath is to secure nothing; it is merely to put a mark of dishonour upon him; it is wanton; and, like all wanton inflictions, it is better repelled by the spirit that defies, than by that which cringes and entreats.

said the professor, 'that I don't know your son; you may conclude he is getting along very well, for if he were a bad boy, I would certainly have made his acquaintance."

The General followed up his little story by an amusing account of an interview he had had with a certain gentleman of Richmond—one of the "Virginia Reserves"—who had strayed into his lines. I must confess his laughter was a little contagious as he gave the details of the interview. The unfortunate individual had come into his lines by some mistake, bewildered as to the points of the compass. His appearance was rather unmilitary, as General B. described it: a suit of black, wet and glued to his skin, a stove-pipe hat, and what seems to have attracted most attention at headquarters, as a curiosity of Richmond—"a black satin vest." "Who are you?" thundered General Butler. "Sir," said the unfortunate individual, with the air of importance in misery, "I am one of the Virginia Reserves." "Alluding only to the oddity of his appearance," said General Butler, I remarked: "and how many more are there like you, Mr. M——?" "I will answer all proper questions," replied the unfortunate individual; "but, sir, General Butler, do not expect me to inform you as to our military resources." The General seems to have thought the old gentleman a little stilted, and explained to me that he only wanted to have a little fun out of him. So, with what I can imagine to have been the growl of an ogre, he remarked: "Ah, ha, Mr M——; so, so, Mr. M——; we have another name than that of soldiers for persons in your dress; yes, sir, another name: we call them SPIES." At the mention of this dreadful word, the unfortunate proprietor of the satin vest went off into protest—pledging "his honour," "his sacred honour," "his honour, which no man, General Butler, had ever doubted;" that he was "a soldier."

I could not help thinking, despite the ludicrous in this interview, the representative of the Richmond second class "melish" had shown the spirit of a gentleman in his replies, and that, even if his dignity was overdone, his sense of honour was apparent through it all.

In the course of conversation, General Butler took occasion—which I believe he seldom omits—to compliment President Davis. He said, "I have a great respect for his ability—a very great respect, sir"—tapping his forehead with his finger. "I voted for him in the Charleston Convention, you know; and I think he has made poor return for old times in calling me 'a Beast.'"

He hoped that Mr. Davis would carry out the policy of arming the slaves on his side. He (Butler) had several thousand "black boys" in his army—he would not say how many—and he would like them to come in contact with black soldiers on the other side. He would be glad to try the experiment. He thought that if President Davis really entertained the idea of using the negroes as soldiers, he should have put it into effect as a *military measure*, instead of trusting to the legislation of Congress. The North would never have armed the negroes if it had been left to the Congress at Washington; but the military leaders took the initiative, and Congress had to follow.

The General said he had in his military department sixty thousand negroes absolved from their condition as slaves. I asked if the negro men who escaped into his lines generally enlisted. "Very generally," he replied. "They do so for two reasons. It improves their social status. And then the soldier's life is attractive to the negro; for though there are in it some hours, and, perhaps, days of tremendous exertion, yet there is plenty of stagnant leisure in which the negro indulges his disposition to laziness."

"To think," said the General, assuming a meditative air, and directing his gaze, *non æquis oculis*, to the ceiling, "how history repeats itself. In San Domingo we had each party eventually arming the negro on their respective sides, and finally the negroes driving the white men out, and taking the country for themselves. But it is scarcely possible the sequel can be reserved for us."

The subject was dropped, as the orderly announced a colonel in waiting. I rose to go. "Never mind," said General Butler; "it's only a visit of ceremony." After a brusque salutation, General B. asks, "how is your regiment, Colonel?" "Flourishing, sir," responded that officer; "but I must tell you, General, I have some officers in my command who are wholly unfit for their positions." "Report 'em to me, sir," said the General; "report 'em to me, and I'll have them examined at once. But you must remember one thing, Colonel: if there is good material in any of them, you must be patient with them; but if there are any crooked branches that you can't get a straight staff out of, I will soon dispose of them, sir."

After the withdrawal of the Colonel, the General called one of his aides, and recommended him to take care of me during my necessary detention at headquarters. I must acknowledge that to this officer—Lt. De Kay—I am indebted for much kindness, and a delicacy of manner I had hardly expected. During the two days I was detained at General Butler's headquarters, there were several occasions on which Lt. De Kay conversed with me politely on many indifferent topics, but never once on military matters. I recollect but one point of comparison he ever made between the beligerents; and it was that "in Richmond there was one thing better than they had in the North, and that was Zarvona smoking tobacco."

I returned to Fortress Monroe—*where I little knew what awaited me!* As the boat passed City Point a man was pointed out on the wharf. He was in plain military dress, was round-shouldered, had his arms swung behind him, and was moving about in a very careless and unsoldierlike gait. I was told it was General Grant. I was not near enough to observe his features.

.... In what I have written above of General Butler's manner and his self-defences—with simple severity of justice—the reader may conclude with me that, like his popular prototype, he is not as black as he is painted. It is not too much to say that he is scarcely worse than other Yankee Generals, and infinitely better than many of them. Compare his career, in which individual outrages stand out, and in which there is much that is merely passionate, and, perhaps, more of fume and bluster than actual performance with the systematic cruelties and cold snakish hypocrisy of Sherman, and we must admit that the sentence of outlawry which President Davis has visited upon the former, is at least invidious. But after all, that sentence of outlawry was *brutum fulmen* intended merely to play a part in our President's elaborate melodrama of retaliation—a mere pretence to turn just popular indignation into the channel of gloomy abstractions and sentimental vapours.

CHAPTER XVII.

ON PAROLE IN FORTRESS MONROE—A Recollection of General Fitz Lee—A Bitter Disappointment—Letter from a Catholic Mother: *In Memoriam.*

I returned to Fortress Monroe, and reported there to Captain Puffer, of General Butler's staff, who enlarged me on parole to the limits of the fort. I was assigned to a scantily furnished, but quite tolerable room; was allowed to hire the attendance of a servant; and thus, in circumstances, certainly not physically uncomfortable, was left to await, with what patience I could command, General Butler's convenience to send me through his lines, on an obligation of honour to make my own exchange in Richmond.

I was treated very kindly by the officers in Fortress Monroe. Many of the men looked black enough at me, and sometimes as I passed a group of soldiers they would strike up their popular army air, "Rally Round the Flag," singing, I thought, with peculiar gusto the line—

"Down with the traitors and up with the flag!"

But this amused me. In no instance was I treated by any of the army officers I met in Fortress Monroe, either insolently or indelicately. One of the officers in the fort, on a certain occasion, invited me into his quarters, gave me an excellent supper, and offered me a bed in his casemate. He was not a "Copperhead;" he never once discussed the war in his conversation; he showed the spirit and sense of a gentleman. He said that, for himself, he had always determined to treat prisoners of war with all the kindness in his power, since an evidence he had had that such conduct was fully appreciated and repaid in the South.

He then told me that when General Fitzhugh Lee was a prisoner in this fort, the officers had treated him with great kindness, for which he expressed his gratitude. Some time after, one of these officers, who had gone to the field, was taken prisoner and conveyed to the Libby. General Lee heard of it, went to the prison, had him unconditionally released, and offered to supply him with any money he might need for his necessities. It is pleasant, indeed, to notice some passages of kind deeds, some mutual recognitions of noble and humane courtesies in this dark and horrible war.

I see from the newspapers that General Butler has gone to Wilmington, and I have heard nothing of my promised exchange. I have had a *curious intimation* that I am not to be exchanged, and that another fate is reserved for me! What does it mean! I have been turned over by Captain Puffer to Major Cassell, the provost marshal; and he cannot or will tell me nothing, although he is not surly or unpleasant when I speak to him. My disappointment is painful and gloomy enough; it treads so closely upon my dearest hopes; it means whatever I may choose to imagine in the way of horrour, as there is no limit to whatever disposition the Yankee authorities may choose to make of a prisoner. Once within a few miles of Richmond, almost in sight of its spires, I find myself turned back, not, as it would now appear, to endure a brief delay, but probably again to go over a long, dreary course of a prisoner's trials—a prisoner's disappointments.

I have received some melancholy tidings, sadly associated with a name that has become ever precious in my prison memories. A letter from an excellent Catholic friend lies before me, telling me of a sore affliction in the family of that gentle Boston lady, whose name there is scarcely a prisoner in Fort Warren can speak without the grateful effusion of his heart. He writes:

"Your dear friend in Boston wrote me a lovely, touching letter the other day, which I wish you could see. She announces to me the death of one of her daughters, of typhoid fever, a few weeks ago—not the lovely girl, with the soft brown eyes, who visited you last summer, but the younger sister. The account she gives me of the dying hours of this dear girl are so touching that I could not refrain from tears, as I read the beautiful story. She died in delirium, imagining herself among the Angels, and chanting with her dying breath the glorious anthems of her Church. The mother is a saint in this lower world—such angelic resignation, such child-like submission, such glorified acquiescence to the blow, which has smitten her to the dust, is a lesson for all who mourn."

And this bereaved mother, in the midst of her affliction, hearing of my prolonged detention as a prisoner, is able to write, for herself, to me words of consolation and encouragement, and to take into her grief the paltry sorrows of a friend. "I bear," she writes, "your burdens with my own. In doing battle with my own grief, I do not forget yours. But for our deep-lying trust in God's infinite love and mercy, how could we bear our trials. To me the perpetual missing of a bright and beautiful presence—the yearning for that which has gone forever—would be unendurable, but that my whole being believes in the infallibility of His love, who has smitten me. Let us both, dear, suffering friend, look our sorrows in the face, and make of them angels to guide and guard us. I have asked my darling, who was so deeply interested in you, and who is now an angel in Heaven, to pray for you, where prayers are efficacious..... There stands near me a most beautiful and touching engraving from Albert Duree, of the Crucifixion—a gift from a valued and dear friend. Look at it with me, my suffering brother! Listen to the voice so full of pathos, that utters the "Father forgive them." Catch upon your aching heart the wail of the blessed Mother, "Oh, all ye that pass by the way, attend and see if there is any sorrow like unto my sorrow." Behold—"*stabat juxta crucem Jesu mater ejus.*" Before this blessed symbol of eternal love, I will daily kneel and pray for you, my friend, that by the Cross and Passion of the Crucified you may be delivered."....

A deep shame mingles with my sympathy in reading these lines—shame for myself that I should be so weak in my own sorrows—so slight in comparison with those of that dearest of friends, who can write such a commentary of submission on her own great affliction. May God forgive me, and arm me for all future time, that in its trials I may have no more words of weak and cowardly complaint, but strength to suffer all things in his Providence! To the afflicted mother, who has been truly a mother to me, and who was wont to call all my countrymen, who were prisoners, "her children;" to her, the Beautiful, who now liveth among the saints in Heaven, my heart shall ever turn for refreshing draughts of grateful memory and holy thought, to cheer me on whatever remains of the weary course of life.

IN MEMORIAM.

Had earth no charms for thee,
That thou, sweet soul, shouldst take the dusty way?
Did love not light thy steps with constant ray,
From tend'rest infancy?

. .   Couldst thou no beauty see,
But such as mock'd thy purest maiden dreams?
Hill, forest, field, and day's revolving beams,—
Were these not fair to thee?

Or did thy spirit crave
Those other fields, where flowers forever blow,—
That many-mansion'd house, whose gate, we know,
    Is narrow'd to the grave?

Were there not hearts whose gore,
For thee, would trickle to the last faint beat?
And hands to scatter flowers about thy feet,
    Along life's rugged shore?

Hadst thou no lot below?
No chord responsive to earth's varied song?
No kindred feeling with the gath'ring throng
    That crowd the courts of woe?

There's joy—high, holy joy
Reserved for those who labour and believe,—
Ear cannot hear, eye see, man's heart conceive,
    Nor envious death destroy!

Such now is thine! Then why
Should sombre grief sit brooding on the soul,
And all the waves of sorrow o'er us roll?
    For thee, 'twas gain to die!

Oh yes! for thee, 'twas gain:
'Twas bliss for thee to feel the fatal dart!
'Tis we alone who press the wounded heart,
    And mourn the cureless pain.

And earth for thee had charms,
And flowers of joy and beauty ever new;
And constant love stood by thee, pure and true,
    To fold thee in her arms.

For these thy soul did glow,
And forward glance, with youth's aspiring gaze,
To sweet home scenes, calm joys, and length of days—
    All worth and love bestow.

And thou wert fair and young,
And bore from time no wrinkle or decay;
But cast thy robes aside, and took thy way,
    To dwell the saints among!

Whilst yet thou tarried here,
The world had one great joy for us who weep;
Now thou art passed beyond the sapphire deep,
    'Tis Heaven alone is dear!

CHAPTER XVIII.

CLOSE AND SOLITARY CONFINEMENT.—Life in a Guard-Box—Memorable Sufferings—A Glimpse of Hope.

I was not left long to imagine the cause of my detention at Fortress Monroe, and the nature of the fate in reserve for me which it implied. Two or three days after I had noticed in the newspapers General Butler's departure down the coast, the provost-marshal came into my room. His air was embarrassed, and when he commenced conversation by saying that "the office of provost-marshal was a peculiar one, and that he had sometimes to do unpleasant things," I was prepared for his next remark that he had "bad news" for me. There was a sharp fear at work in my heart—one of those moments of keen anxiety when a few words are to determine the fate of a man—as I answered with a constrained calmness that wrung my nerves, that I appreciated his kind and polite words, but knowing very well that he was bound to execute his orders, I was ready to accept my fate whatever it was. He stated that I was sentenced to *close and solitary confinement*; and that he had been so instructed by a telegraphic despatch *from General Grant!* And this then was the issue of all my hopes; this the trap into which I had been taken; this the monstrous violation of the faith of the Washington Government; for I had come to Fortress Monroe under the protection of a parole, which Secretary Welles had never rescinded, and which I certainly had never compromised, and under the protection, too, of a special official order of the same Secretary, directing me to go forward "to be exchanged." What could such perfidy and cruelty mean? I could not easily attribute it to Secretary Welles, after his former honourable treatment of me; I could still less imagine it to have proceeded from General Butler, who had so recently and so distinctly promised to send me through his lines. Had any charges been made against me? What had General Grant, who was in no way connected with the exchange of prisoners, to do with me? Major Cassell, the provost marshal, could tell me nothing but what was in the text of his orders.

This officer had been very gentlemanly to me on all occasions. He was kind in his manner now; but it was useless to waste questions on blank politeness. I asked him if he could spare me the ignominy of a cell, and he suggested that I might be confined in a guard-box, near the sally-port. If I had chosen the cell I would have been far more comfortable than in the wooden box allotted to me, where there was no room to walk in, and where, for many days and nights, coiled under one blanket, I was to lie shivering in the cold winter air that ventilated my shell of boards.

The narrow door was closed upon me by the officer of the guard. I had remarked to him that General Grant was probably acting under some misapprehension with reference to me. He replied that "General Grant did not go out of the usual way in the treatment of prisoners, and he supposed I was held as a spy." I shuddered to find as he passed out that double guards were placed over me; in addition to the sentry a few paces off, at the sally-port, another being placed immediately at my door. I heard him remark to a comrade that he had "a spy in there whose neck he hoped would be soon broke."

I ran over in my mind swiftly all my past life in prison and on parole. Surely there was nothing in it on which to hang the least charge against me, or of which even the most ingenious conspiracy could avail itself, as long as I kept cool enough to cope with the machinations that evidently sought to take my life, either by a stroke of cunning, or by the torture of a prison unparalleled save in those damp unhealthy cells of the Bastile, where the victim of despotism was left to die quite as surely as by the axe of the hangman. I quickly concluded that I was not held as a spy, but was designed as the victim of some malice in Washington as yet unexplained, which was conveniently seeking my destruction, and by cutting me off from the world and surrounding me with an air of mystery, was attempting to consummate it *in silence*.

It was a terrible thought to languish in a wooden box like a dog—perhaps to die there in silence! For a moment I felt like turning upon my face, and and abandoning all to despair. But it was only for a moment.

The experiences of life are of but little use, unless one gathers in them the resources of resolution. I had learned something from the past. I had recently prepared myself by reflection for whatever trials might await me. I had recovered my health on parole; I had gained flesh and spirits; and never in my life was I so thoroughly armed at all points for a test of my resolution. In ten minutes I had looked my situation in the face and thoroughly made up my mind how to act. If I thought or sulked in this place I would easily die. I determined that my mind should not feed upon itself; that I would find constant occupation for my hours; that I would invent trifles to kill time; that if I could not use my legs, I would jump up, toss my arms, do anything that might serve for exercise under difficulties. And then I would be constantly on the alert to effect a communication with my friends to discover and defeat the enemy who was responsible for this outrage upon me, and to break the mesh of malice in which my fate seemed now to be so mysteriously woven.

My first task was to get the permission of the provost-marshal to write to General Grant. I stated the circumstances of double protection in which I had come to Fortress Monroe—that of a parole granted by the Secretary of the Navy, and that of an official order under which I had reported; I desired to know why the faith of the authorities implied in these steps had not been kept with me; I asked simply what charges had been made against me. The letter was never noticed.

And here I may say that I wrote three letters to the same effect to General Grant in one week. Not a word of reply. I was again to learn the lesson that the Yankee authorities have the same convenience as that of the Bastile—that is to keep the prisoner in profound ignorance of his fate, and leave him a prey to imagination.

It was a bitter reflection what a return I had obtained for my own rigid and punctilious observance of faith with the enemy. When first captured and taken to Boston, I was invited to escape, and it was suggested to me that on a technical construction of my parole to go to Boston, I was free when the vessel touched the wharf. I put the suggestion from me as an unworthy one, and surrendered myself to the United States Marshal. The thanks I got for it was that he attempted to put me in the common jail. Again, while on parole in the streets of Boston, there were men who said to me "put yourself in our hands, and in twelve hours you will be safe in Canada; we want you to go to England, and carry out your designs, and you have only to name what amount of money you will need and it is yours." I answered these Boston sympathizers: "You do not know how we in the South regard matters of personal honour. Unless I can go back to Richmond with clean hands, I will never return there." The thanks I got for this was three months in Fort Warren. Again put on parole, I had conducted myself, as Secretary Welles admitted to one of my friends, in an unexceptionable manner, and I had never provoked the remark of a newspaper, or drawn the attention of an official in three months of comparative liberty. My reward for such observance of the faith I had pledged in my parole of honour, was that without any known charges, without explanation, and in what I supposed was the last stage of my exchange, I was caught up by a telegraphic dispatch, and doomed to a fate little short of death—that of close and solitary confinement in a space where there was not room to take two steps."

But I was determined not to chew the cud. I was but a few hours in my narrow prison—my little stall of boards—before I had divided off the waking hours of the day into employments, petty enough, but which might serve to kill time by method. I had a needle and thread in my valise, and might sew. I had a knife, and might whittle. I had a book which had been thumbed and studied over, but I might find a pastime, and an exercise for the lungs in reading it aloud. I had the stump of a pencil and some loose paper, and I might amuse myself with making rebusses, puzzles, and perhaps poetry. But I had made no calculation for the dark hours of the night, and did not imagine how little of these could be appropriated to sleep; for the temperature of the day afforded me no imagination of the sufferings I was to endure, shivering in the cold air of the night that swept through my frail tenement, catching sleep on my eyelids for five minutes at a time, and dreaming horrible dreams of naked and shelterless misery.

.... Days, weeks I passed in solitary confinement, without a word of communication from human lips. Part of this time, my sufferings were intense. My limbs were cramped in the narrow limits of my prison; they were pierced with cold; I could not stand on my feet without a feeling of giddiness.

I never shall forget the bitter, bitter cold of Christmas week. In shivering wakefulness during the long hours of the night, I could hear the guard trotting up and down before my door, with the thud of his heavy accoutrements, keeping company with his double-quick in the freezing atmosphere. It was some night in the last of December, when the officer of the guard opened the door, no doubt curious to see the condition of his prisoner since three weeks of solitary confinement. I was huddled under a blanket, with some extra articles of dress strewn over it. The officer was not without humanity, for he seemed to be shocked at my condition. "Well," he said, "a man don't know what he can stand! I am a stronger man than you, and I am certain that I could not live in this place two weeks." He said, "I will remonstrate with Colonel Roberts, and see if you can't be made more comfortable." He promised to send the surgeon of the fort to see me next day. The surgeon came, examined my condition, and declared that he felt bound for humane and sanitary reasons to advise a change for me, both of quarters and of discipline, and would try to get me permission to walk an hour each day under guard. I never heard a word more from these officers; I never saw them again; I suppose that if they did make the appeal they promised, it was rebuffed. I had requested them if they could learn anything of my sentence to request in my behalf that it might be commuted to any sort of penal labour—the Dry Tortugas, the penitentiary—anything was preferable to the crouching, shivering, solitary confinement in a wooden box! Nothing came of this request. I was left in silence; alone with my imagination.

It was in the early part of January, 1865—I cannot recollect the day of the month—that peering through a crack in my wooden box, I was surprised to see General Butler driving out of the sally-port in an open barouche. It was a glimpse of hope, for I had taken in it a sudden conception, and had made a quick calculation of probabilities. I instantly judged that General Butler had returned from Wilmington, and was on his way to the Richmond lines. Ascribing my incarceration to some influence at Washington, and having obtained, some time before, an intimation that a quarrel was existing between General Butler and the War Department, and that he and Stanton were acting in opposite directions, the idea at once came into my mind that that quarrel might be turned to my benefit, and that my prompt and adroit use of it might probably open my way to liberty.

I took a scrap of paper on my knee, and instantly wrote to General Butler, reminding him of his promise to send me through his lines, and suggesting that his authority in this matter had been superseded and defied in a manner inexplicable to me. I directed the note to "Headquarters Army of the James," and handed it to the corporal of the guard. He kept it out about two hours, and then returned it to me, saying the officer of the day would not allow it to pass. I assumed an air of great indignation; I said, "I'd let General Butler know how communications addressed to him on official business were treated by subordinates;" I demanded that I should see the provost-marshal instantly about what was quite as much an act of disrespect to General Butler as of outrage to myself. The provost-marshal was sick. But his assistant came, and instantly pacified me by taking the letter, and promising that General Butler should have it in the next twelve hours.

In that letter I had got in my hand the clew to undo the web of malice that had been woven around me.

CHAPTER XIX.

A WEEK IN THE YANKEE LINES AROUND RICHMOND.—The Pleasure Party on the "River Queen."—General Butler Aroused and Profane.—Yankee "War Correspondents" at Headquarters.—Material of the Yankee Army: Negro Soldiers.—Yankee Officers on "Subjugation."—General Butler's Tribute to General Lee.—How I Made a Narrow Escape to Richmond.

There is little ceremony in the liberation of a prisoner. Two days after my note to General Butler, the provost-marshal opens the door, and tells me to "pack my things in ten minutes." He does not tell me why; he does not state where I am going; the old mystery of the Bastile is kept up to the last moment. But I do not ask any questions this time; for I know very well that General Butler is taking action over the heads of Grant and of his master at Washington, and that it is my policy to keep a discreet silence.

A sergeant marches up to take me in custody. As I step into the open air my cramped limbs tremble under me, and I stagger, giddy but pleasantly bewildered, towards the wharf. There was lying General Butler's staff-boat, "the River Queen," gay with flags and streamers; in its upper saloon groups of gaily dressed ladies, among them the wife and daughter of General B., on a pleasant jaunt to the front, for the benefit, as I afterwards learned, of a party of English naval officers, whose lustrous uniforms added to the picturesqueness of the scene. As I approached this garish boat, on which I was told I would be taken under guard to General Butler's headquarters, I found groups of women at the windows of the saloon taking that cool survey of me, some with the assistance of lorgnettes, that only the impertinent curiosity of Yankees could bestow. I had always made it a point when a prisoner, to put on the best appearance before the enemies of my country. Before I had left the fort I had found time to cleanse my face and hands, and to dress myself with the most scrupulous care; and I thought I detected in the curiosity, which proposed to feast itself on the spectacle of a rebel prisoner, a shade of disappointment that there were no appendages of interest to me in the way of rags or clouts.

I held myself carefully aloof from the company on the boat. Several of the English officers on board seemed to make it a point to walk near where I was standing; and I could plainly see sympathy and interest in their looks despite the restraints of the Yankee company whose guests they were. There was no breach of manners in what they did; although I could plainly read in their eyes a feeling which made me proud and flushed to know that it reflected an admiration for my country, testified to a plain, solitary man, who stood under guard in a throng of Yankee pleasure-seekers—a stark figure of a prisoner, in the midst of the gilt and revelry of his enemy.

My second interview with General Butler did not last three minutes. It was refreshingly brief. Arrived at his headquarters, I was ushered by the provost-marshal into his presence.

"Sir," said General Butler, "I understand you have been put in confinement since I paroled you and promised to send you through my lines. I had nothing to do with it, sir. Read this."

He handed me a paper. It was a telegraphic dispatch *from Secretrry Stanton* to General Grant, ordering me into close confinement. The mystery was revealed; I saw the demon at the bottom of it; I had calculated aright my appeal to General Butler as my only hope of escape.

I handed the paper back to General Butler. He twirled it between his thumb and forefinger. "By G— I don't know what this means. I don't care what it means. I believe, Mr. Pollard, I promised to send you to Richmond."

"You did, General Butler."

"By G—, sir, you shall go. I would send you through my lines to-morrow. But I sent a flag-of-truce down the road the other day, and some of your people fired upon it. They must have been d—d drunk."

He rose from his chair as a signal for the conclusion of the interview. "Sir," he said, "I always keep my word, alike to friend and foe. I know 'hope deferred maketh the heart sick;' and you may yet be detained here a week for Colonel Mulford's flag-of-truce, but make up your mind that go you shall to Richmond."

I replied that his assurance completely satisfied me. I could scarcely suppress my feelings at the prospect before me. I would defeat Stanton's plot; I would override him and get back to Richmond. But to effect this, I saw *the value of silence*, and the paramount necessity of doing or saying nothing to draw the attention of the Washington authorities upon me, and to bring to close quarters a quarrel through which my hope was to slip unperceived.

I was turned over by the provost-marshal to the staff-quartermaster, who assigned me a bunk and invited me to his mess. This officer—Lieut. Merrill—was both civil and kind. But there were some civilities in store for me that I had not expected.

I had scarcely entered the quartermaster's hut when an orderly came in with a full file of New York papers, which he handed me, accompanied by a card, on which was written "Compliments of James B. Chadwick, New York Tribune." In a few minutes after this surprise another card was handed me, on which there was this prolix designation: "S. Cadwallader, Correspondent-in-Chief New York Herald, General Grant's Headquarters, Armies of the United States." Presently a fat gentleman, in a heavy suit of quadrangular stripes, who introduced himself as another correspondent of the Herald, invited me to a large double hut, assigned to the representatives of the press permitted to reside at headquarters.

I found here about a dozen "war correspondents" of different Northern papers in an atmosphere of tobacco smoke. There were liquors, nuts and raisins on the table; excellent Havannas, *ad libitum;* and a retinue of black servants in attendance—for the Yankee "war correspondent" is an important personage at headquarters, keeps his horse and servant, and receives a salary scarcely less than the pay of a Major-General. I was treated with abundant hospitality. But I must not venture to describe the festive relaxation of my polite entertainers; for the fat correspondent of the Herald, who treated the company to several scenes and reminiscences of his on the comic stage, seemed to be nervously afraid that I was "taking notes," and made me promise, in the most solemn manner, "not to put him in the Richmond Examiner."

There was one piece of gentlemanly delicacy in a passage of general conversation of the company that I could not fail to appreciate, and should not neglect to mention. Two of the company were engaged in quite an animated discussion of General Butler's merits, when one of them got upon the slavery question. Mr. Chadwick, the representative of the *Tribune*, immediately interferred, and said: "Perhaps such conversation is not pleasant to Mr. Pollard; let us change the subject." No one but a gentleman could have shown such a ready sense of propriety.

I parted from my entertainers with many protestations of their desire "to see me in Richmond," and the rather dubious declaration that if the Yankees got there I would certainly be "looked up."

Six days in the Yankee lines; and I have learned some things which will bear repetition.

I wish every man in the South could see for himself the extent of the deterioration of the material of the Yankee army. He would find in this view an encouragement for the Confederacy that had not before entered his mind; and when he saw on what legs the war is now supported in the North, he could readily understand the peculiar difficulties of Yankee recruiting, and how they are verging to the last necessity.

I had an interesting occasion of observation within the Yankee lines around Richmond; I had had for several months an insight into the recruiting offices, with which the City Park, in New York, is shingled; I had, on different occasions, had the freedom of the city of Boston, which is the great entrepot—much more so than New York—of foreign enlistments; and when I declare to the reader that the proportion of citizens of the United States in the Yankee army has fallen to about one-fifth of it, and these the worst and nastiest "scabs" of Northern cities, he may be sure I am not amusing him with extravagant assertions, but giving him the results of careful and reliable information.

Foreign enlistments, as is now well known, have got to be in the worst odour in Europe, and that source of supply of the Yankee army may be said to have pretty thoroughly dried up. Negro soldiers are now at an immense premium at the North, and yet they are obtained with the greatest difficulty. I saw a negro in the hotel at Fortress Monroe who had escaped from Richmond, and whom I had known in a Main street restaurant; and he told me that he had no sooner put his foot on the passenger boat, which runs from Varina to Washington, than he was taken hold of by a pack of bounty agents, and that one Massachusetts man offered, if he would go to Boston and enlist as his substitute, to give him $900 cash outside of the bounty. "Moses" couldn't see it. The "smart" negroes do not enlist.

General Butler had much to tell me of his success in the experiment of negro soldiers. But outside the views of the negro question by General Butler and other Northern negrophilists, I have made my own observations. The most invariable, and perhaps the most important of these is, that the black soldiers in the Yankee army are mostly composed of the dregs of the negro race; that of escaped slaves, those who enlist are generally nothing more than the ignorant and uncouth plantation "scrubs," who can find no other employment; and that this black element in the armies of our enemy, if it is to be considered at all, may be taken as almost beneath contempt. A Yankee officer told me that negro soldiers were found to have an animal abhorrence of the sight of blood; that in some charges they had been, as soldiers often are, pushed on blindly; but that if they once catch sight of mangled limbs and spirting blood, their imagination is at once shocked, and they are utterly demoralized.

To see these miserable creatures in the lines about Richmond, standing up to their haunches in mud, and rolling their eyes like lost spirits, gives one a very curious idea of the material of the army which General Lee confronts. The white element of that army is only a degree better. I may say, that in all my enforced intercourse for many months with privates in the Yankee army, I have never heard from them any sentiment of "Union," any echo of articles in the newspapers, any expression of so-called "patriotism;" their whole stock of conversation and employment, besides studies of obscenity, is to tell what they have made in bounties, and to count the days when their terms of enlistment will expire. If the veterans of the Confederacy are not able to smash up such material, black and white, as the Yankee army now takes into its composition, they might as well give up their occupation and go home in disgrace. The Confederate public can have no idea of the utter deterioration of this material since the campaign was opened in last May. It is such in the armies of the Potomac and the James, that I candidly believe if General Lee had good reason to assume the aggressive, he could break their lines around Richmond from one end to the other.

The fate of Richmond, should the Yankee flag ever float over it, I am not left to imagine. I had heard that fate already decided in every Yankee circle of discussion. But while within the lines of the enemy's armies around Richmond, I obtained an expression of the designs of those who, more than the politicians, are to give law to the conquered.

It is possible that there may be some few fools who imagine that in Richmond, under Yankee rule, they might go on in the old established routine of their lives, leaving politics alone. Never was delusion more false or fatal. It is perfectly agreed among the Yankees that if Richmond should ever fall under their domination, a test must be applied to it far more severe than has ever yet been enforced upon any portion of the Southern people; for it is this city which is regarded as the headquarters of the rebellion, and it is here where the Northern grip is to strangle "treason." It is certain that no one could breathe in the atmosphere of Richmond unless he swallowed the oath of allegiance in its vilest form. If he saved his property for a few days by that step, he would yet be given over to ultimate ruin. He would find Richmond inundated with men who would be his masters in everything; Yankees would keep the hotels, publish the newspapers, sell the dry goods and "notions." He would be turned out of all employment, unless he might get that of clerk or understrapper to some "go ahead" New Englander who wanted cheap help. He would be kept under constant surveillance, and at the mercy of every enemy who might choose to tell a lie about him to the Yankee provost marshal. Life would become intolerable to him. From Richmond to the farthest corner of Virginia he would find the places of himself and his countrymen usurped by the Yankee; and even if he saved himself from the jail by oaths of allegiance, repetitions of the old feudal "homage," or any other expedient of infamy, he would find himself pushed to the wall and regarded as an incumbrance and superfluity upon the earth.

I found more instruction than entertainment in the talk of the Yankee army about Richmond. I had access to many of its officers, who spoke of the war without reserve. And this talk was an unfailing ding-dong of what Yankee enterprise would do in Virginia after its subjugation. Virginians didn't know how to cultivate the soil; the Yankees would give them a lesson; the old estates would be cut up into 100-acre farms to give every man a chance. Some had new methods of raising tobacco, as they had seen it done in the Connecticut valley. Some thought the Valley of Virginia the most inviting country in the world, and had picked out their places to settle there after the war. This talk was not intended to be offensive; for it seemed to be universally taken as matter of course that under Yankee rule, Virginia, by a very fair, logical conclusion, could be for nobody else but the Yankees, and that her former people were to be glad to sit at the feet of New England civilization.

———

An officer on General Butler's staff told me that whatever denunciations of Confederates Butler might have indulged in, he had a great admiration of Gen. Lee. He related a singular story to illustrate it. He said that some time ago General Lee had exposed himself on a line of earthworks, within musket fire of one of Butler's regiments. Some of the officers thought the men who recognized him should have shot him. Butler said his soldiers had done right not to fire on him—that he would think it "a crime against humanity to take the life of such a man as General Lee." Now this may have been affectation. But what must be the general estimation of the worth and virtues of the man, who could give occasion, even, to an affectation of this sort from the lips of an enemy!

———

On the 10th of January, it was known at the headquarters of the army of the James that General Butler had been relieved from all command, and ordered to report at his home in Massachusetts. The news was a terrible surprise to me. The flag-of-truce under which I was to be exchanged had not yet come up the river. General Butler's authority was at an end; and I had reason to suspect that if in any way it became known at Washington that I was *en route* for Richmond—that if any application for instructions in my case was made to any new authority, the probability was I would be intercepted, and consigned again to the horrors of close and solitary imprisonment. A terrible anxiety was upon me. But I saw at once that my only hope was to conceal it. If the provost-marshal was to telegraph to Washington for any instructions about me, the probability was I was lost. I knew he was but little aware of the circumstances of my case. I conceived at once the part I was to play. It was constantly to speak of my going to Richmond under the next flag of truce as a matter of course; to avoid the least suggestion of any conflict of authority in my case; to have nothing stirred; to talk confidently of my intended departure as a thing already fully determined and settled in every respect. Each morning at breakfast I made it a point to say, "Well, I suppose I will sup to-night at the Spotswood." I promised the provost-marshal to send him back from Richmond a bale of smoking tobacco. But while I thus spoke with the appearance of easy and good-natured confidence, my heart was gnawed by a terrible anxiety. I knew very well that my fate hung by a thread.

My success was even beyond my expectations. Without the least ado, without question of any sort, I was on the morning of the 12th January informed that a flag-of-truce was in the river, politely and comfortably placed in an ambuance, and in one hour was at Boulware's landing on the boat that was to convey me to Richmond. I did not feel safe until the provost-marshal who had accompanied me to the boat had taken his leave; which he did very pleasantly, little dreaming that the prisoner he had put through so graciously was supposed by the authorities at Washington to be groaning in solitary confinement at Fortress Monroe.*

How can I describe my feelings as thus narrowly escaped, as it were, from the very jaws of destruction, I stood once more beneath the flag of my country, and saw lifted into the evening sky the spires of Richmond! That night I slept the sweet sleep of one returned to his home. And that night my heart long pent up with anxieties poured out, happily and reverently its gratitude to God.

---

* I arrived in Richmond the 12th of January. Some weeks afterwards I received by the flag-of-truce mail a letter from a friend in Washington, addressed to me "in prison at Fortress Monroe," and forwarded from there, giving an account of an interview at the War Department about my case. This letter was dated the *sixteenth day* of January. It said:

"My Dear Friend: I have been here for two days, exerting myself to procure some amelioration of your condition, but *utterly without success*. Secretary Welles, a humane, benevolent man, and a thorough gentleman, expresses regret at your circumstances, but says he has delivered you over to the War Department, and has no control whatever over your case. He very generously gave me permission to use his name in my interview with the Secretary of War, and to say he (Mr. Wells) had sent me to Mr. Stanton. I went to the War office yesterday. Mr. Stanton has gone to Savannah, so that I had to see the Assistant Secretary, Mr. Dana. Although I was accompanied by ———, his manner to me was such as to *forbid my again appealing to him*. Indeed, he very promptly and imperatively told me NOTHING COULD BE DONE FOR YOU."

This news of Yankee determination to keep me in close and solitary confinement—to let me rot in prison—I read, on the very day it was uttered, a free man in the streets of Richmond!

CHAPTER XX.

Some Reflections.—The Hope of the Confederacy.

February 20, 1865.—Some weeks before the publication of these pages, the writer returned to his home in Richmond with a feeling of exultation in his bosom, and bringing with him the deliberate and firm conviction that in the affairs of the North there were elements of encouragement for the South such as no former period of the war had contained. He found this opinion, for some time, doubted by many of his countrymen, and but few of them willing to catch the inspiration of any idea which lies beyond the immediate impressions of the hour. Nor is this altogether strange. It is true that the elements of encouragement referred to may not be appreciable in a hasty examination of the situation, or they may have been sunk out of the popular view, while it has been too much occupied with the superficial regard of reverses and mishaps to our arms.

It is true that we have had a series of misfortunes and misadventures in the military field. Yet count these altogether since August last, and the sum of actual results, although in favour of the enemy, is not the least occasion to us for despair. We still cover the vitals of the Confederacy with powerful armies. The passage of the enemy through Georgia did not conquer that State. Hood's defeat in Tennessee leaves the situation in the Central West about what it was in 1862, after the battle of Shiloh. The capture of the forts in the Bay of Mobile has not given that city to the enemy, or even given him a practicable water base for operations against it. The fall of Fort Fisher simply closed the mouth of a river. The march of Sherman may, by a defeat at any stage short of Richmond, be brought to thorough naught; the whole country which he has overrun be re-opened and recovered, and nothing remain of his conquests but the narrow swath along the path of the invader.

This is all of the dark side of the situation for us; and when we estimate how much of it is to be attributed to the fact of incompetency on the part of our Generals, and how much of it may yet be repaired or compensated by a change of commanders, and in that new era of military administration upon which we are now entering, when campaigns are no longer to be dictated and commands assigned by the caprice and obstinacy which have heretofore governed all things in Richmond, we may well take courage for the future, and count the military disasters of the past as things very far from decisive results, and even, in any view, not past the reach of timely and vigorous remedies.

We state all that there is to discourage us at present, when we make the enumeration of misfortunes to our arms since the midsummer of 1864. There is another side to the account to be looked at before we strike the balance. There is a certain peculiar and extraordinary encouragement for us in the military affairs of the North at present, which we have not before experienced in the history of the war, and which much overweighs all our recent misfortunes in the field.

It was stated by the writer in other pages of this work that the public mind in the North was not disposed to carry the war beyond a certain point of distress and necessity, which it had already nearly approached. When a nation fights for empire there is a limit to its endeavour very far from positive exhaustion. When a nation fights for existence, there is, there should be, no end to the struggle but in the extinction of all its resources. The North has made up its mind not to fight past certain necessities. The South should make up its mind to fight to the last necessity. The war has resolved itself into a simple question of endurance on the part of the South; and the time has come when an exhibition of the spirit of the people in that respect is more important than a victory in the field.

The Union sentiment in the North is a curious and interesting study after four years of war. There is no candid man in the North but will tell you that that sentiment has declined since the commencement of the contest, because, as the war has progressed, the realization of the Union "as it was" and the restoration of the former order of things have become more and more impossible to the hopes and views of the intelligent. But whatever the explanation of this loss of fervour in the Yankee mind, one has only to go through the North at this present time and mix with the people, to discover that, whatever may be the rallying cries of parties and the rhetoric of the newspapers, "the Union," has fast fallen from its first estimation as the indispensable thing of the Yankee, his *sine qua non* in the war, to the condition of a mere preference in the popular mind—a preference which, so far from its being impossible to overcome, is already weak and halting at the prosect of further endurance on the part of the South.*

The dreaded **necessity of** a conscription must **now** soon be upon the North. To this necessity, **to** a repetition of this necessity, **when** the South, by her endurance, forces her enemy, she accomplishes **arguments** against the war more effective in the present disposition **of** the Yankee mind than any which the experiences of the war have ever yet afforded. There **are** already signs of the hunger for peace in the North, such as have never yet been exhibited. It is in these symptoms **of** a declining war; in the embarrassments and distress of a Yankee conscription; in the new value given to the simple quality of *endurance* on the part of the South, that our people may discover an encouragement which they never had before in the history of their great contest.

No one can doubt that the South has yet great capabilities of endurance: the question is merely that of the disposition of the people to exert them, in good faith, and with a firm purpose. There has never yet been any real scarcity of subsistence in the South, although our resources in this respect have been mismanaged. There has not been a year since the commencement of the war in which there has not been an actual *surplus* of production in the South. Our scarcity of men and resources are, alike, unreal. Our armies can yet be doubled by the mere reclamation of absentees in a new era of military discipline, far more important than any enlargement of paper legislation. Our resources of

---

* I have found among men in the North who are not fanatical a very general admission that the reconstruction of the old Union is a Utopia. They give this opinion: that the so-called Union sentiment may be resolved into a desire for the maintenance of an American prestige and the better cultivation of material interests; and that whenever the Northern people are convinced that what is left to be realized of these objects is only to be accomplished by some sort of league between the North and the South—that this is the only possible remnant of the Yankee desire, they will accept it as such; and that in the settlement of this conviction, the great Question of Peace is logically destined to find its ultimate solution. I add here my own opinion: that the North will take this conviction at some stage of the war very far from the last extremity to which it may be fought out. There seems to be a well-determined conclusion in the intelligent Yankee mind, that if the South should obtain such military successes as should put her in a position in which she was not likely to accommodate the North with any leagues or treaties to preserve the remnant of old interests in the Union, and to insist upon a severe independence without any such connections whatever, that then the South would succeed to the prestige and prosperity of the old government, and the North be utterly ruined. It is thus that I am persuaded that the North will never fight this war to an extremity, or beyond that certain stage of success or certain exhibition of resolution on the part of the South which will give occasion for the development of those opinions to which I have referred.

conscription in three millions of slaves are yet untouched. Everywhere the difficulty is that of mismanagement and neglect, not that of exhaustion. Such a difficulty is only accidental; it disappears when the spirit of the people is thoroughly aroused, and acts with decision. The safety of the South is brought to the simple problem of the public resolution; there is no other uncertainty; there is no other demand. There is nothing else of fear but on this single point; and there is nothing else of hope but on it alone.

The writer does not propose to attempt here any determination of the question of *putting arms* in the hands of the slaves, or any opinion as to how more than three millions of blacks may best be used in our military organizations. But their use in this respect, as a resource in reserve, has its value and its interest; and these we may regard without the incumbrance of details, or seeking to determine what should be the precise employment or status of the negro in the armies of the Confederacy.

In the first American war for independence—that of the Colonies—Edmund Burke then pointed to the black man as the military ally *of his master.* He used a language then to the British Abolitionists, which, after the lapse of nearly a century, we may repeat to-day, almost word for word, to our enemy:

"With regard," said he, "to the high aristocratic spirit of Virginia and the Southern colonies, it has been proposed, I know, to reduce it by declaring a general enfranchisement of their slaves. This project has had its advocates and panegyrists; yet I never could argue myself into any opinion of it. Slaves are often much attached to their masters. A general wild offer of liberty would not always be accepted. History furnishes few instances of it. It is sometimes as hard to persuade slaves to be free as it is to compel freemen to be slaves; and in this auspicious scheme we should have both these pleasing tasks on our hands at once. But when we talk of enfranchisement, do we not perceive that the American master may enfranchise too, and arm servile hands in defence of freedom? A measure to which other people have had recourse more than once, and not without success, in a desperate situation of their affairs. Slaves as these unfortunate black people are, and dull as all men are from slavery, must they not a little suspect the offer of freedom from that very nation which has sold them to their present masters?"

If the negro is serviceable at all as a soldier, he will rather be so under the care and direction and inspiration of a master than as the ally of the Yankee. The South can give him officers who understand him better than those of the enemy can; and she can offer him inducements to courage and good service far more valuable in his eyes than the nominal, wretched freedom of a Yankee Helot. The precise position of the negro in the armies of the Confederacy is a matter of detail—a detail which belongs, as we believe, to a remote necessity. Yet it is encouraging that we have a resource of auxiliaries, no matter if used in the meanest employment of the army, and that with it we can put a weight in the scale of the war that the enemy has not yet felt.

But it may be but little necessary to look to extreme necessities, if we are only resolved to cope with those already upon us, which in a few months may be decisive. Do those men who take our defeat and ruin as a foregone conclusion reflect that we have six hundred thousand white men in the Confederacy capable of bearing arms! Do they know that, despite the shortcomings of conscription, and despite that wretched mismanagement which has wormed holes into everything, and made our army a sieve, our forces east of the Mississippi river to-day number more than one hundred and thirty thousand men, and are, at the lowest estimate, more than three-fourths of the aggregate force of the enemy actually under arms! Did they hear President Davis say in his recent speech at the African Church how Kossuth had been so weak as to abandon the cause of Hungary with an army of *thirty thousand* men in the field! And are we ready to tarnish our reputation, and hand ourselves down to the damnation of history, by surrendering to an enemy, with an army on our side and actually in the field more numerous than those which have made the most brilliant pages in European history.; an army more numerous than that with which Napoleon achieved his reputation; an army standing among its homesteads; an army in which each individual man is superiour in every martial quality to each individual man in the ranks of the invader, and reared with ideas of independence, and in the habits of command! The disgrace of such a surrender would have no parallel in history. If the cause of the Confederacy is lost, it is lost by weak despair; by the cowardice of suicide; by the distress of weak minds. It cannot, CANNOT be lost, if the spirit of the people rallies; if dauntless resolution and renewed energy are put against the small and decreasing advantages of the enemy in other respects. We are very far from the historical necessity of subjugation. We are at any time near the catastrophe of a panic.

In the face of existing resources; with the promise of a new dawn in the administration of our military affairs; with the stirring inspirations of the recent lessons we have had of the fell designs of the enemy to require from us nothing short of the unconditional submission of the vanquished; with the authoritative definition of the word "Subjugation" fresh from the ogreish lips of the Washington Oracle there never was a time less fit to turn our backs upon occasion, and write "Despair" on the banners of the Confederacy.

Let us hope that the period of re-animation thus invoked will come; that the resolution of the people will rise with occasion; that the public spirit will plume itself again for the contest. It is in such revival of the war; in such assurance of the determination of the people of the South to accept new tests of endurance that the enemy will feel a dissuasion from the prosecution of hostilities against which all his recent sensations of military success will weigh as dust in the balance.

The Confederacy may commit suicide; but it will do so when the message of a new hope is on wings to save it. There is somewhere a story of a wretched prisoner visited by the Devil to tempt him to suicide. He was told there was no hope for him; he was urged to end his misery. A step was heard descending to his cell, as the wretched man held the knife at his heart. "Quick," said the Devil, "it is the step of the executioner." The knife was plunged into the bosom; and as the eyes of this victim of cowardly despair swam in death, he saw before them the King's pardon held out to him—knew too late that the step he had heard was of one bringing the message of liberty.

www.ingramcontent.com/pod-product-compliance
Lightning Source LLC
Chambersburg PA
CBHW020101170426
43199CB00009B/358